KU-337-507

The Greeks on Stage

Geraldine McCaughrean is one of today's foremost
children's writers. She is the author of many novels
and classic retellings for children for which she has
won the Carnegie Medal, the Guardian Children's
Fiction Award, the Whitbread Award and the Blue
Peter Award. She lives in Berkshire with her husband
and daughter Ailsa.

The Greeks on Stage is a companion volume to
Britannia on Stage, which presents twenty-five scenes
from British history also in the form of short plays.

Schools Library and Information Services

S00000645175

THE GREEKS
on Stage

25 Plays from
Greek Mythology

Geraldine McCaughrean
Illustrated by Richard Brassey

Dolphin Paperbacks

First published in 2002
as a Dolphin paperback
by Orion Children's Books
a division of the Orion Publishing Group Ltd
Orion House
5 Upper St Martin's Lane
London WC2H 9EA

Text copyright © Geraldine McCaughrean 2002
Illustrations copyright © Richard Brassey 2002

The right of Geraldine McCaughrean and Richard Brassey
to be identified as the author and illustrator respectively
of this work has been asserted.

All rights reserved. No part of this publication may be reproduced,
stored in a retrieval system, or transmitted,
in any form or by any means, electronic, mechanical,
photocopying, recording or otherwise, without the prior
permission of Orion Children's Books.

A catalogue record for this book is
available from the British Library.

Typeset at The Spartan Press Ltd,
Lymington, Hants

Printed in Great Britain by
The Guernsey Press Co. Ltd, Guernsey, C. I.

ISBN 1 84255 034 9

DUDLEY PUBLIC LIBRARIES

L 46150

645175   SCH

J822.

This book is dedicated to all the actors
whose talents succeed in bringing the words to life.

CONTENTS

INTRODUCTION

Here are twenty-five one-act plays – royalty free – from the vast, sprawling, intertwined mythology of ancient Greece. Some, like Icarus and his wings, or Midas with his golden touch, are well known. Others are rarely told but could be equally entertaining on a stage. They are *not* (bar one) adaptations of the great Greek dramatists, but simple dramatised folk stories, happy and sad.

The level of difficulty varies: some can be mounted by juniors studying the Greeks for Key Stage 2, others by secondary students doing drama studies. There is definitely no upper limit, and I shall be sorely disappointed if adults never undertake them.

You will want to pick and choose. For instance, you may want to use the plays singly – at class assemblies or during a cross-curricular week. Or you may want to select ten and create a two-hour performance. The great merit of linked plays is that every member of the cast gets a chance to shine. The poor soul required to be a spear carrier in one scene has the prospect of a starring role in the next. As the mother of a keen actress this was my driving motive!

Unifying pieces of script – ons and offs – are included at the back of the book. I used these as the finishing touches to a show whose first half focused on the gods and whose second half concentrated on the mortals.

I have purposely included some longer speeches here and there, at the suggestion of a LAMDA drama teacher constantly in search of examination set pieces.

Attached to each script is a list of characters, props, costumes and special effects required – but take them with a pinch of salt. We're not all working in an ideal world with limitless resources, and in my experience simplest is often best anyway.

Similarly the stage directions imply a proscenium stage, but most of the plays will work just as well in the round or on the flat. Feel free to tinker with these scripts, cut them, work in suggestions from the cast . . . No published script has ever reached its finished or ideal form.

Lastly, this collection makes no attempt to educate *anyone* in Greek history or culture. Its aim is to mine the fun, excitement, emotion and enlightenment to be had from a good story and from putting on a play.

Geraldine McCaughrean

The Race to Live

The world is complete. But when it comes to creating the human race, Zeus's attempts seem doomed to failure.

Cast

NARRATOR

ZEUS

HERA

APOLLO

PROMETHEUS

GOLD MALE

GOLD FEMALE

SILVER MALE

SILVER FEMALE

BRONZE RACE (4)

IRON RACE, made up of all actors available, including gold, silver and bronze less their costumes

Costumes

- 2 'ponchos' of gold cloth
- 2 'ponchos' of silver cloth
- 4 'ponchos' of bronze cloth

Props

- Zeus's throne 5
- modelling balloons, some previously made up into animal shapes
- thunderbolt (cardboard jag of lightning painted black)
- flat template of Parthenon
- metal tool box containing:
    bits of fur fabric
    chisel and hammer
    metal dross to make lots of noise when moved
- 4 helmets, bronze in colour

Special Effects

- waffle board for thunder
- music, e.g. *The Planets*, during creation of each race

Idea!

How many other creation myths do you know? How many include the gods (or God) scrapping one creation and starting again?

THE RACE TO LIVE

The stage appears empty but for a NARRATOR, *stage front left, and* ZEUS *who sits disconsolately in his throne, centre stage. Three pairs of actors are already onstage, however, concealed by gold, silver and bronze drapes, to look like rocks. There are several model-making balloons tied to the throne. It also has a side pocket containing jagged, lightning-shaped 'thunderbolt' and temple template. Under it is a large metal tool box. Concealed behind it are already made balloon animals.*

(ZEUS *whistles between his teeth, drums his fingers, patently bored. He starts fiddling with the balloons, twisting them together. Passes behind throne and emerges having 'made' a poodle. Shows it to audience for them to admire. 'Makes' a giraffe. 'Makes' a person*)

NARRATOR: It came into Zeus's head one day that he would create a race of people, who would live on Earth and worship the gods with rites and sacrifices – who would build temples and tend shrines.

(ZEUS *eagerly holds up flat template of a Greek temple*)

He wanted them to be special, of course. And so he made them out of gold.

(ZEUS *raises up the two* GOLD *figures and introduces them to each other*)

ZEUS: The Race of Gold!

(*The* GOLDS *walk elegantly up and down*)

GOLD MALE: Exquisite!

GOLD FEMALE: The first and most perfect work of Creation!

GOLD MALE: Look us over!

GOLD FEMALE: Far too precious to stoop to heavy labour. Far too high born to soil our beautiful hands.

GOLD MALE: Quite as fine as the gods themselves, in fact.

> (ZEUS, *about to sit down, starts up again, shocked at what he is hearing*)

GOLD FEMALE: The question is, who is going to fetch and carry for us?

GOLD MALE: Who is going to worship us or build statues of us?

> (ZEUS *snatches up the thunderbolt and strikes dead* GOLD MALE *and* FEMALE)

ZEUS: (*aggressively, to audience*) So I scrapped the Race of Gold and began again.

> (*During the* NARRATOR's *speech,* ZEUS *raises the* SILVER *figures to life*)

NARRATOR: This time he used silver – the colour of the moon. The finished effect was lovely – like moonbeams dancing on the sea.

> (SILVER MALE *and* FEMALE *briefly dance about the stage. They are very New-Age and vacant.* ZEUS *is entranced*)

SILVER MALE: We are *very* spiritual.

SILVER FEMALE: We sense at once what the gods want of us, and do it.

> (*They pray, bow and meditate*)

SILVER MALE: In fact we are *COOL*. Very cool.

SILVER FEMALE: Totally unstressed.

SILVER MALE: Children of the glimmer.

SILVER FEMALE: From the borders of Sleep.

ZEUS: Cool!

SILVER MALE AND FEMALE: *COOL!*

(*Sleepier and sleepier, they sit down and fall fast asleep*)

ZEUS: But once they fell asleep, they were inclined to stay that way.

HERA: (*entering a short way from wings*) For good and always. A bit of a design fault, if you ask me.

ZEUS: (*touchy*) They were just a prototype.

(HERA *winces as* ZEUS *'rolls' the* RACE OF SILVER *off stage with an immense kick. Rattle of thunder.* APOLLO *enters, striding energetically on stage*)

APOLLO: Zeus started again. This time with bronze.

ZEUS: I buried the Race of Silver and I used bronze instead – the kind of metal well suited to tools and utensils.

(*He gouges the* BRONZE *figures out of the stage with his thunderbolt. They are wearing Greek helmets and breastplates.* BRONZES 3 AND 4 *enter from the wings*)

BRONZE 1: (*loud and strident*) We were no sooner made than we were manufacturing.

BRONZE 2: Saws and chisels and hoes and spades.

(*They mime using these tools*)

ZEUS: Splendid!

BRONZE 3: And axes and sickles and ploughshares.

ZEUS: Excellent!

BRONZE 4: And daggers and shields and javelins.

BRONZE 2: And swords and spears and clubs.

ZEUS: What?

BRONZE 3: And hammer.

BRONZE 4: And tongs.

(*The* BRONZES *set up a taunting chant,* 1 AND 2 *against* 3 AND 4, *swelled by* APOLLO *on one side and* HERA *on the other*)

BRONZES 1 AND 2: Hammer!

APOLLO: Tongs!

BRONZES 3 AND 4: Hammer!

HERA: Tongs!

BRONZES 1 AND 2: Hammer!

APOLLO: Tongs!

BRONZES 3 AND 4: Hammer!

HERA: Tongs!

ZEUS: *STOP!*

APOLLO: But the Race of Bronze had no sooner finished hewing and building than they turned their energies to making weapons and killing each other!

(*Mayhem breaks out among the* BRONZES. *The* GODS *try to restrain them but they break free and go back to wrestling, sword fighting, throwing punches. They even punch the* GODS *by mistake. One by one, the* BRONZES *fall down dead or groaning wounded*)

ZEUS: (*sitting down in throne, disgusted, head in hands*) I didn't have to destroy these ones. They did it for me. By the time they—

BRONZE 1: (*wounded but still aggressive*) Hammer!

BRONZE 4: Tongs!

(*Dies*)

ZEUS: By the time they had finished, I had to start all over again.

HERA: But what are you going to use?

APOLLO: All the gold is buried underground.

NARRATOR: All the silver, too.

HERA: And the bronze.

(ZEUS *drags from under throne his tool box. Holds up scraps of fur, then the balloon poodle, etc.*)

ZEUS: I have some fur left over from making the animals! It may have to be . . .

APOLLO: Achilles the Poodle.

HERA: Odysseus the Ocelot.

NARRATOR: Perseus the Platypus.

ZEUS: Unless . . .

(*He bends down as if to pick up a handful of earth but is revolted by the feel of it*)

Where's Prometheus! Call Prometheus the Titan.

(*The* 'HUMAN RACE' '*roll*' *on stage as* PROMETHEUS *enters. They remain curled up in balls.* PROMETHEUS *bows*)

PROMETHEUS: You called, Lord Zeus?

ZEUS: Yes. I have it in mind to make a new race of creatures and to make them from the rocks and clay. They say you are a craftsman – good with your hands. Mould me something, in the likeness of the gods . . . Not too beauti-

ful, mind! And not too grand. Not too clever and not too
dangerous. A humble, useful sort of a species.

(PROMETHEUS *bows again, crouches down and
'moulds' the curled-up figures into people. The* PEOPLE
uncurl first an arm, a leg, etc., then stand up)

ALL: The Race of Iron!

ZEUS: (*dismissive of* PROMETHEUS, *taking the credit himself*) Yes. I shaped the fourth race— All right, Prometheus,
thank you, you can go now. I shaped the fourth race out of
iron and clay.

HERA: Not very beautiful.

APOLLO: (*in a thickly stupid voice*) Not very bright.

ZEUS: But *very* superstitious – terrified, from the moment
of their birth, of disappointing us gods.

(PERSON 1 *sees* PERSON 3 *and they begin to kiss and*
embrace passionately)

And self-propagating!!

(*Gradually all other members of cast drift on stage*
chattering about trade, prices, children, schools, rela-
tions, aches and pains, omens, bad luck . . .

ZEUS, *finding he can no longer see the audience, pushes*
his way through to stage front. He has to speak louder
and louder above the din)

In time, they multiplied. In fact, in time, there were soon so
many of them that every hill, every island, every shore of the
central sea, had a temple or a shrine to the gods, burning
incense, chanting prayers . . . (*Winces and puts his hands*
over his ears) Although the noise could be a little trying. (*To*
HERA) Are you sure this was a good idea of yours, Hera?
(*Looks into the audience*) Look at them all down there. The
Race of Iron. Ah well, if we ever run short of horseshoes, we
can always recycle them, I suppose . . . QUIET!

(*Roll of thunder. The* PEOPLE *onstage look round at*
him in fright, then, as he and the other GODS *exit stage*
left, instantly go back to what they were doing, and
exit, chatting, stage right. The NARRATOR *joins them*)

Stolen Fire

The people of Earth are cold, hungry and miserable, but fire is one gift the gods are determined to keep to themselves.

Cast

HE

SHE

PROMETHEUS (should be tall)

5 (or more) other MORTALS

ZEUS

HERMES

HELIOS (optional)

HERA

POSEIDON

2 GUARDS

2 (or more) DANCERS

Costumes

- Gods and mortals as elsewhere
- Prometheus slightly grander than the mortals

Props

- 2 electric log-effect fires
- tin plate
- green tablecloth
- toasting forks and crumpets
- blankets
- coil of rope
- cuffs and chains (mock)
- a stem of straw (e.g. barley)
- 'eagle' gloves
- large orange helium-filled balloon
- 'chained' dummy dressed like Prometheus
- several small torches

Special Effects

- Thunderclap

Idea!

This is an exercise in stage lighting, but how would you manage to tell the story without it? Work out how to portray light and fire and warmth without it being there. The 'black-out' at the beginning could well be depicted by the actors 'acting blind' (as in Michael Frayn's *Black Comedy*).

Note

This play is the 'prequel' to *Pandora's Box*, but either play will stand alone. In a collection of plays including *Breaking the Bonds* 289 the model Prometheus remains throughout, until Herakles brings the story to its close.

STOLEN FIRE

Black-out (if possible).

Two tables stand in diagonal corners of the stage: (A) rear stage left, (B) front stage right. On table (A) is an electric coal-effect fire (not yet lit). Another fire waits in readiness offstage right. A green tablecloth lies folded on table (B). The dummy and chains lie across rear of stage hidden by hem of backdrop curtain. The GODS stand motionless around table (A) holding crumpets on toasting forks. HE and SHE are not visible. Their voices emanate from the dark. SHE obviously has a streaming cold.

HE: Are you there?

SHE: I'm here.

HE: Where's dinner?

SHE: On the table in front of you, of course.

HE: I can't see it.

SHE: Well, feel about for it . . . but be careful.

(Noise of tin plate falling to floor and rolling on its rim round and round. Pause)

HE: Whoops.

SHE: You wouldn't have liked it anyway. It was liver.

HE: Urgh. You know I hate liver.

SHE: I hear it's nice . . . cooked. Are you still there?

HE: Of course I am. Where could I go in this dark? *(Pause)* I'm cold.

SHE: Want another blanket?

HE: Couldn't we huddle together for warmth?

SHE: Certainly not! You know what would happen. (*Pause*) You'd catch my cold. (*Sneezes*) It's all right for the gods.

(*The electric fire on table (A) is lit and the* GODS *come to life, tasting crumpets, looking cheerful and chattering. The stage lights come up.* HE *and* SHE *are revealed looking miserable and huddling under blankets*)

ZEUS: Pass the ambrosia, Hermes.

HE: Must be lovely having Fire.

SHE: (*miming*) Your own little sliver of sun.

HE: (*miming*) Holding a flame on the end of a stick, like a juggler balancing plates.

SHE: Bright as moonlight in the dark – only warmer.

HE: Turning meat from rubbery blubber into crackly melting deliciousness.

(*Both sigh then kneel down and direct prayers towards the* GODS)

BOTH: Please! Oh please! Gods of Olympus, share the secret of Fire with us!

GODS: (*variously*) Fire? Huh! / What an absurd idea! / The cheek of those mortals! / Let *them* loose with fire? Imagine the damage they would do! / Is there no end to the airs these people give themselves?

HE: I'll take that for a No.

SHE: What we need is a hero – a champion – a demi-god. Someone who cares about underdogs like us.

HE: I'm hungry. Where's that liver?

SHE: I think the cat's got it.

(*Both drop down on hands and knees and feel around.*
HE *crawls off stage. Spitting and squeal of outraged cat*)

HE: Ow! Somebody stepped on my hand!

(*Enter* PROMETHEUS *wearing climber's rope*)

SHE: (*feeling* PROMETHEUS*'s knees*) Ooo. He smells nice,
whoever he is. Sort of big and strong and— ooo, what's
that?

PROMETHEUS: That's my rope. I'm a climber. I wondered
if I might be of service to you.

(*Momentary freeze, then* SHE *gets up briskly, spreads
cloth on the table and mimes serving a meal and drink*)

SHE: When morning came, we could see him for what he
was – an absolute giant of a man. In point of fact . . . (*looks
furtively over either shoulder*) . . . a Titan.

PROMETHEUS: My brother is Atlas the giant – you may
have heard of him. My younger brother – Epimetheus –
lives hereabouts.

HE: And you say you're willing to try and *steal* Fire from
the gods?

PROMETHEUS: Hardly steal. How can you steal a thing
and it still be there after? I just think that Mankind ought to
share in the blessing. Fire wasn't invented by the Olympians, you know. So why should they keep it all to
themselves? Listen. When the world was new, and Zeus
was making people to inhabit it, he was ready to work with
gold; he didn't mind silver. Even bronze. But when it came
to soil and water . . . Well, he gave the task over to me,
sooner than get his hands dirty. So I mixed mud, and I
moulded them: (*miming*) first Man and first Woman. The
prototypes, anyway.

HE: That was *you*?

PROMETHEUS: Uhuh. I gave them the best of each of my earlier designs – the pride of the lion, the dexterity of the monkey, the courage of the eagle, the laughter of the jackal . . . Trouble is, of course, you make a thing, you tend to love it. I don't care that Zeus took the credit. But I *do* care that he oppresses you – hems you round with duties and rules and rituals. Now take Fire . . .

SHE: Oh, if only we could!

PROMETHEUS: The gods keep it to themselves, while the little people I made have to sit shivering around tables of raw food and cold water!

SHE: But if they caught you, Prometheus! What would they do to you if they caught you?

(*More* MORTALS *drift on stage from right*)

PROMETHEUS: I don't know. Salute my daring? Who knows. Who cares. Who wants to come with me?

ALL MORTALS: Where?

PROMETHEUS: Up to the sky, of course! To the top of the highest mountain, somewhere where the sun chariot scuffs its chariot wheels as it drives across the sky! Somewhere I can reach the Sun!

(*They gawp at him, and drop back upstage, too terrified to go with him*)

MORTALS: (*variously*) Steal from the gods? / We wouldn't dare! / Ambush the sun chariot? / Not in a million years! / The best of luck to you, Prometheus! / The gods help you!

(*They turn to the person who has said this last speech and round on her*)

He's on his own.

(All *chant*)

Up, Prometheus! Higher! Higher!
Fetch us down a piece of Fire!

(They repeat this while PROMETHEUS *climbs up onto table (A) and stands, straw in mouth, looking noncha-lant.*

Enter HELIOS *(or other) with a big, helium-filled, orange balloon, which he 'walks' across the stage, allowing it to rise higher at the centre then decline downwards in a parabola)*

GODS: *(taking a line each)*
Across the sky gallops the Sun god's chariot,
evaporating clouds from the morning sky,
bestowing its heat on the fields below.

MORTALS: Up, Prometheus! Higher! Higher!
Fetch us down a piece of Fire!

GODS: Straight and true it steers its selfsame daily route
from the Gates of Dawn towards the Stables of Sunset
setting the dewponds glittering,
crimping shadows to the cows,
wetting the harvesters with sweat

MORTALS: Up, Prometheus! Higher! Higher!
Fetch us down a piece of Fire!

(The MORTALS *run off stage)*

GODS: Gold-leafed with flame, it drops out of the noonday sky
down across mountain peaks so high and desolate that no one . . .

ZEUS: *(calling across the stage) Stop!* Who goes there?
Prometheus, is it? What are you doing there?

(PROMETHEUS *shrugs, sucks straw, spreads innocent hands*)

Did you touch the fiery chariot just now? I saw you reach up . . . Hermes! Search him!

(HERMES *runs and frisks* PROMETHEUS)

What are you about, Titan Prometheus? Sabotage? Theft? Were you trying to pluck the sun chariot out of the sky?

PROMETHEUS: Not at all, not at all.

ZEUS: Or copy it? You are a great *maker*, I seem to remember. A great modeller.

HERMES: Nothing on him, my lord.

ZEUS: Very well. You may go. But if I find . . .

(*Exit* PROMETHEUS *with a bound of pent-up delight and energy*)

Hmmm. Titans. You never know where you are with Titans.

(*Goes back to toasting crumpets.*

HE, SHE *and the other* MORTALS *burst on from right, arguing and anxious for* PROMETHEUS's *safety; they end up strung out across the stage. Each holds, concealed, a small torch, unlit*)

MORTALS: (*variously*) He didn't. / He can't have. / I'll bet you he did! / Zeus would never allow it! / He could never get close enough.

(*Enter* PROMETHEUS. *All the* MORTALS *shout at him*)

DID YOU GET IT!?

(*He keeps them waiting a moment then takes the straw from his mouth and holds it up*)

HE: It's in there?

SHE: Hidden inside a stem of grass?

(PROMETHEUS *passes in front of them, 'lighting' their kindling, so each is left with a palmful of light and delighted face*)

PROMETHEUS: No saying where you got it, mind.

(*Exit* PROMETHEUS, *finger pressed to his lips*)

MORTALS: (*calling after him fervently*) Thank you, Prometheus!

(HE *and* SHE *go back to their corner and 'light' the electric fire to toast crumpets exactly like the* GODS. *The others scatter to all parts of the stage*)

HERA: What's what? A glow worm?

HERMES: A firefly.

POSEIDON: A shooting star. Or a flying fish catching the sun.

ZEUS: No it's not! . . . It's Fire! The Race of Mud have stolen the secret of Fire!

(*General outrage among the* GODS)

When I find out who did this . . . he'll pay with an everlasting torment!

(*Clap of thunder. All* MORTALS *cower down, looking at* ZEUS *who ranges raging about the stage*)

Who did this? Who stole from the gods? Who went against the will of Olympus? Who helped you discover the secret of Fire?!

MORTALS: (*pointing   cravenly   offstage*) IT WAS PROMETHEUS!

(2 GUARDS *wrestle* PROMETHEUS *on stage*)

ZEUS: So. Prometheus. What have you to say for yourself?

PROMETHEUS: That the world is finally full of the smell of woodsmoke – as it should be. That at last ships can find their way safely into port. That the statues in your temples have shadows now, even at night, and the sweet smell of herbs burning under their marble noses. What's wrong, Zeus? Are you jealous of your own creation? See how the lights multiply. The whole Earth is aglimmer with campfires – like the stars reflecting in an ocean. Every house. Every travelling caravan. Every window—

ZEUS: You'll pay for this, Prometheus! I'll make you sorry you were ever born, let alone helped these mud men to defy the gods. Take him away! Chain him to the Caucasus Mountains!

(*The* GUARDS *fetch, out of either wing, long silver chains with cuffs, and chain* PROMETHEUS *by the*

wrists. They move out to the end of the chains, so that
PROMETHEUS *is held, centre stage, in a position
reminiscent of the Christ crucified. Black-out.*

Exit PROMETHEUS. *The miniature dummy is now
strung up, on small-scale chains, against the backcloth
where it remains throughout the performance)*

(*As lighting returns*) Let eagles peck out his liver by day,
and by night let it regrow, so that his torment may last from
everlasting to everlasting.

(DANCERS *with feathery gloves persecute the dummy,
pecking at its reddened chest*)

HE: What have we done?

SHE: He did it all for us!

MORTAL 1: And now he'll be tormented for ever!

MORTAL 2: No mortal hand can break the chains that bind
him.

MORTAL 3: No mortal weapon can beat off those eagles.

SHE: Must he suffer for ever, for taking our side? Oh,
Prometheus, we will pray for you always!

MORTAL 4: Oh, Prometheus, we will always love you more
than we love the gods!

MORTAL 5: Oh, Prometheus, it will always be your face we
see in our forges and hearths and campfires.

ALL MORTALS: (*chanting together*) Zeus is a bully. Zeus is
a tyrant.
Zeus was jealous. Zeus was afraid.
Zeus has a heart of stone.

PROMETHEUS: (*from off*) Do you hear them, Zeus? Do
you hear them? Our little people of mud?

ZEUS: I hear them, Prometheus. And they'll pay, too: don't

think they won't. Soon they will be feeling so sorry for themselves that they'll have no pity to spare for you. (*Calling*) A box! Bring me a box. A big box. I have *so* many things to fit inside. So many *presents* for Mankind. I'll send it to your brother, Prometheus. To Epimetheus and that new wife of his. What was her name again? Ah yes, *Pandora*. (*Exit calling*) A box, I say! For Pandora!

Pandora's Box

Why send a wedding present and then forbid the
newlyweds to open it?

Cast

NARRATOR

PANDORA

EPIMETHEUS

PAIN

ENVY

WORRY

SICKNESS

ANGER

SORROW

OLD AGE

DEATH

HOPE

Costumes

- short bridal veil for Pandora
- short white tunic for Epimetheus
- masks for Evils

Props

- large cabin trunk with back cut away
- confetti
- posy of flowers
- vase
- window (can be held up by two of the Evils)
- black piece of cloth on thin string
- walking sticks for Old Age
- butterfly on wire stalk

Special Effects

- pre-recorded speeches or handheld amplifier to project whispering voices inside the trunk
- graveyard music

Ideas!

Make papier mâché masks representing the various Evils. What movements will best express their different characteristics?

Compare this myth with the myths of other cultures explaining the existence of evil, pain and death in the world.

PANDORA'S BOX

This set assumes curtains at the rear of the stage, centre-stage back. Covering a join in the rear curtains stands a large fibre-board trunk, its back removed to allow actors to enter it from behind the curtains. It has been covered with an ornamental throw.

NARRATOR: Zeus is no longer so fond of his Race of Iron. They are too noisy. They are too ingenious. They are too *durable*. However rugged and wild, the world is so beautiful that the gods are almost envious of the people who live there.

No matter. Early days. And creation is not quite over yet . . .

(PANDORA *and* EPIMETHEUS *enter laughing, amid a shower of confetti thrown from offstage. She wears a small bridal veil and holds a posy of flowers*)

PANDORA: Oh, Epimetheus! What a wonderful, wonderful day! All those people! All that dancing! I don't believe there ever was such a wedding.

EPIMETHEUS: Well no. Probably not, my sweet. It was the first ever.

PANDORA: Oh, I'm so happy! Just think, Epi! You and I together for ever in this beautiful place – in this ravishing world! Nothing to do but pick fruit off the trees and gather flowers and cook for our friends and love each other and— (*She breaks off, seeing the trunk*) What's that?

EPIMETHEUS: It's a wedding present.

PANDORA: Oh! Ooo! Let me see! Let me! (*Pulls the blanket off*) Who sent it? When did it come? What's in it?

EPIMETHEUS: Nothing. No. Come away. It was a gift from Zeus himself. It came this morning. It's a trunk. It's nothing. Leave it alone.

PANDORA: I can *see* it's a trunk, silly! From Zeus? Wow! It must be something really marvellous! What's inside? . . . What's this? (*Reads ticket*) DO NOT OPEN? What, until he comes visiting? What does it mean, Epi? 'Do not open'?

EPIMETHEUS: It means just what it says, darling. Zeus was quite specific. We are not to open it. Those were his instructions.

PANDORA: What, not for a week? Or until our first anniversary? When?

EPIMETHEUS: Not at all. Ever. Is that so hard to understand?

(*He snatches the blanket back and re-covers the trunk*)

Just do as you're told and leave it alone, there's a good girl. Ignore it. Forget it. Pretend it's not there.

PANDORA: But I only want to—

EPIMETHEUS: Pandora! Do as I tell you. Am I not your husband?

(*They look at each other, standing nose to nose, then* EPIMETHEUS *breaks away*)

I must go and help Silenus get home. He's drunk too much wine ever to get there under his own power. Remember now. Stay away from the trunk.

PANDORA: All right, Epimetheus.

EPIMETHEUS: Promise?

PANDORA: I promise.

(*Exit* EPIMETHEUS)

It's only a stupid old trunk, anyway.

(*She straightens the cover*)

Who cares about some old trunk.

(*She fetches a vase and puts her posy in it, arranging the flowers restlessly. Pauses between each phrase*)

Probably just sheets and blankets.
Or pots and pans.
Stuff.
Old files and papers. They must make a lot of paperwork on Mount Olympus. (*To audience*) Don't you think?

EERIE VOICE: Pandora!

(PANDORA *decides her ears are playing tricks on her and ignores it. The voice comes louder*)

Pandora!

PANDORA: (*to someone in the audience*) Was that you?

EERIE VOICE: Pandora! Open the trunk!

PANDORA: No! I mean – I mustn't! Who are you? Epimetheus said . . . Zeus said.

EERIE VOICE: But what about *you*, Pandora? You want to, don't you?

PANDORA: Shush! Don't. I mean – you'll have to wait till Epi comes back. He'll explain. I don't understand why; I just—

EERIE VOICE: Oh, but Pandora, we can't wait till then! We need you to help us! We need you to let us out! Now!

PANDORA: There are more than one of you in there? No!

(Steps away and turns her back on the trunk, not knowing what to do)

EERIE VOICE: But that's not fair on you, Pandora! After all, it's your present as well as his! You heard him. 'Do as you are told, Pandora.' Is that how it's going to be from now on? You ought to show him. Just because you're married, are you going to let him order you around like that?

PANDORA: *(mimicking* EPIMETHEUS*)* 'Leave it alone, there's a good girl. Am I not your husband?' All the same . . . Should I?

(She appeals to the audience for advice)

Should I?

EERIE VOICE: Don't listen to them! What do they know? What are they doing in your house anyway? Oh, all right, then. All right. Don't open the trunk . . . But one little peep. How can that hurt? Don't open the trunk. Just lift the lid a crack. Take a peep. You wouldn't believe what Zeus put in here! You *know* you want to, don't you? Please. Please. Pleeease, Pandora! Do it, do it, do it, do it! We can't breathe in here!

*(*PANDORA *very cautiously opens the locks, then the lid a crack. It is knocked out of her hands and thrown open by the actor inside.*

As each actor climbs out, the next wriggles in through the back, so that the trunk appears to hold an impossible number of people. Each in turn prances and cavorts (attracting attention away from the trunk), then rushes off stage to either side or clambers out through the window. Masks could represent their characteristics.

First out is PAIN, *who rises to full height, confronting* PANDORA. *Not immediately obvious whether good or bad. Stretches itself)*

PAIN: Free at last!

   (*Suddenly slaps* PANDORA *across the face*)

I am PAIN! Feel me, Pandora?

ENVY: I am ENVY!

   (*Tours stage, coveting everything from the vase to* PANDORA's *dress, saying, 'Oo, I want that', 'Oh, I wish I had one', etc. Steals* PANDORA's *wedding veil and runs off wearing it*)

Eat your heart out, Pandora!

WORRY: I am worry. Oh dear. Oh dear. Oh dear, oh dear, oh dear! Anxiety, that's me. Fret and Regret. Worrying, isn't it, Pandora?

SICKNESS: And I . . .

   (*Crosses to flower vase and crushes the flowers one by*

one. A piece of black cloth is pulled out of the trunk on
a string and tugged off stage)

I am SICKNESS! There goes my brother BLIGHT!

WORRY: Oh Pandora, what have you done?

ANGER: (*raging, fists up*) Who are you looking at? Don't
you recognise me? I'm ANGERRRR! Wanna make something of it? Just wait till I infect your husband. Think how
angry he's going to be with you for what you've done.

SORROW: (*emerging*) Think how sorry!

(*Runs weeping and wailing into the body of the theatre,*
touching people as she goes and shouting back towards
the stage)

I am SORROW! How the world will thank you for setting
me free, Pandora! Free to blind every eye with tears. Free to
nest in every heart I meet!

OLD AGE: Or me! Old Age! The blight of every pretty
cheek! The marring of even the most perfect beauty.

(*Has great difficulty in getting out of the box with*
walking sticks. She almost falls. PANDORA *goes to help*
her and OLD AGE *battens on her, rubbing chalk into her*
hair, until PANDORA *drives her away.*

Seeing what is coming next, PANDORA *tries to shut the*
trunk lid, but DEATH *forces it open, too strong to be*
resisted)

DEATH: (*amplified voice*) And I am DEATH!

(*Grabs* PANDORA *round the throat and dances with her*
to graveyard music)

What a wedding gift you have given the world, Pandora!
Death, disease and pain, envy, misery and anger. Oh, nicely
done, Pandora! Nicely done! Ha ha ha!

(*Throws* PANDORA *to the ground and exits. She drags herself to the trunk, shuts the lid and hauls herself across it to keep it shut*)

HOPE: (*amplified whisper*) Oh, Pandora, let *me* out! Don't leave *me* inside, whatever you do!

PANDORA: Shut up! No! Do you think I'm stupid? You don't catch me the same way twice!

HOPE: Oh, but Pandora! Without me, Life will be unbearable!

PANDORA: No! I told you, no! I won't let any more of you out!

HOPE: The monsters you have loosed will eat up every heart. The world will be paralysed by despair! Let me help, Pandora! Let me out!

PANDORA: (*to audience*) What should I do? NO!

(*She goes to the window*)

Haven't I done enough? See? The trees are all withered. The fruit is cankered. The people crying. Smoke from the funeral pyres. Haven't I done enough? Oh, Zeus! What did we ever do for you to hate us this much?

HOPE: Pandora! Let me out!

PANDORA: (*shrugs despairingly*) Why not? There's nothing left to lose.

(*She throws open the lid and takes hold of the handle of a wire stalk, on the end of which is a paper butterfly. She flutters it round the stage, enchanted by its prettiness*)

HOPE: (*amplified whisper*) I am Hope! Never lose sight of me! I am your only Hope!

(PANDORA *collides with* EPIMETHEUS *who enters with*

ANGER *crouching behind him, pulling tongues at*
PANDORA *as if he has snitched on her*)

EPIMETHEUS: What have you done, Pandora?

PANDORA: Oh don't be angry! I'm sorry, Epi! I didn't
mean to! Ask them. (*Indicates audience*) It's our wedding
day, Epi! Our wedding day!

EPIMETHEUS: Do you seriously think there can be any love
between us after what you've done today?

(HOPE *settles on his shoulder*)

PANDORA: Oh there can, Epimetheus! There could be!
. . . At least . . . I hope so.

(EPIMETHEUS *relents.* ANGER *withdraws sulkily*)

EPIMETHEUS: I hope so, too.

(*She runs to him and they hug, an embrace of consolation rather than passion, then exit*)

The Golden Chariot

The boy Phaethon is spoiled. When he gets his way once too often, it seems the world will be spoiled too – or utterly destroyed.

Cast

HELIOS, the sun god

CLYMENE, his wife

PHAETHUSA
LAMPETIE } their daughters

PHOEBE, a younger daughter

PHAETHON, their son

ZEUS

ARCTIC GROUP
DESERT GROUP
SEA GROUP
PANIC GROUP } about 3 in each group

Costumes

- Zeus as elsewhere
- gold-fringed costumes or flame-coloured sashes for Helios and family

Props

- the front of a chariot, free-standing
- carriage whip with clip for fastening to chariot
- four long leather reins
- lightning-shaped thunderbolt

Special Effects

- sound effects of clip-clopping, galloping, neighing (optional)
- sound effect thunderclap or waffle board

Idea!

This story has a lot to say about ecology and our need to look after the planet responsibly. You might like to insert a speech of your own, to this effect.

THE GOLDEN CHARIOT

The front of a golden chariot stands mid-stage with four reins running over the edge of the stage to some tethering point. There are three people asleep in each corner of the stage: ARCTIC GROUP, DESERT GROUP, SEA GROUP, PANIC GROUP.

(*Enter* HELIOS, *striding manfully towards chariot, pursued by* PHAETHON *who darts round him, also* CLYMENE (PHAETHON's *mother) and his sisters,* PHAETHUSA, LAMPETIE *and* PHOEBE)

PHAETHON: Oh please, Father! Please let me! Let me, let me. I can do it! I know I can.

HELIOS: No.

PHAETHON: Oh pleeease! Please, please, pretty please! I know I can do it.

HELIOS: Phaethon, no. I said no, and I meant no.

CLYMENE: Stop pestering your father, Phaethon. I don't know: once you get an idea into your head, you're like a dog with a bone.

PHAETHON: (*whining*) But why not? Why can't I? I want to. I'd do it just the way you do.

HELIOS: Driving the chariot of the Sun is a skilled job, son. It calls for delicate hands, careful handling. My horses are powerful beasts.

PHAETHON: (*aside*) Blagh. Anyone could do it. (*Showing biceps*) They wouldn't give me any trouble. I'm strong, Father. Look at that. Feel that! I'm strong!

PHAETHUSA: He is strong, Daddy. That's a true thing.

HELIOS: That's enough, Phaethon! No, I said. No. You must learn to take no for an answer.

CLYMENE: (*indulgent*) Maybe when you're older, son.

PHAETHON: (*sulky*) What difference will that make? Father won't get old and die! He's an immortal. So when do I get my turn? It's not fair.

LAMPETIE: Phaethon is very clever, Daddy.

PHAETHUSA: He is very good with horses!

PHOEBE: (*to her sisters*) If he can't, he can't. Can we not leave it at that? He's too young.

HELIOS: Will no one ever give me any peace? Nag, nag, nag. Nagging me day and night, picking away at me like an unravelled seam. 'Let me drive the chariot, Father', 'Let me steer the sun chariot, Father', day in, day out, wheedling and whining. You're like a mosquito buzzing in my ear sometimes, Phaethon! Perhaps I should . . . (*Raises his hand as if to swat*)

CLYMENE: Oh, Helios, no! Don't! What are you thinking of! Our own dear boy!

PHOEBE: Phaethon is spoiled. He has to have everything now.

CLYMENE: You hold your tongue, Miss!

PHAETHON: Yes. You keep quiet, you. (*Back to wheedling*) I'll do just as you tell me, Father. I've watched you a thousand times!

CLYMENE: Oh go on, Helios. Just this once. It would give the boy such a thrill.

PHAETHUSA AND LAMPETIE: Yes, Daddy, let him have a turn.

HELIOS: (*exploding into a tantrum*) Agh! Am I never to have any peace? All right! Do it! Do what you like! Let him kill himself! Let him crash the Sun! Darken the firmament for ever! Wind my finest horses! What do I care? I'm only the Charioteer of the Sun, after all. I'm only the Celestial Charioteer! Why should I expect my own family to obey me? Who am I to expect any respect?

(*Throws reins at* PHAETHON *and makes as if to exit*)

Go on! Drive it! And if you get into difficulties, don't say I didn't warn you!

(PHAETHUSA *and* LAMPETIE *skip about with glee, while* PHOEBE *looks worried.* PHAETHON, *smugly gratified, pulls a face at* PHOEBE *and gets 'into' the chariot*)

CLYMENE: (*pleased*) Oo now, Phaethon, you're such a naughty boy, vexing your father like that.

PHAETHON: Stand back! Keep clear of the wheels! Here I go! Phaethon, the Shining One, Charioteer of the Sun!

HELIOS: (*turning back, suddenly anxious*) Remember, now – keep their heads straight forwards. Keep looking between their ears. Fix your eyes on the western stables, and keep your height steady and your speed even.

PHAETHON: Yes, yes, yes. Here I go! Do you see me, Mother? Driving the chariot of the Sun?

CLYMENE: (*waving*) I see you, dear! Take care, now!

PHOEBE: He has to have everything he wants, the very moment he wants it.

HELIOS: (*shouting now*) And don't use the whip! I never use the whip! (*To himself*) I only use the whip for show.

PHAETHUSA AND LAMPETIE: Look at baby brother! Up there on his own, in the chariot of the Sun!

PHOEBE: Take care, Phaethon.

(*Sound of clip-clopping. Exit* CLYMENE, PHAETHUSA *and* LAMPETIE. PHOEBE *stops, extreme stage left,* HELIOS, *extreme stage right. They watch* PHAETHON)

PHAETHON: (*clicking his tongue*) Gee up, there! Get along, you lazy nags. You may only trot for my father, but I'm Phaethon, Charioteer of the Sun. (*Looks over side of chariot*) Wake up, you lazy little mortals! Can't you see the Sun is rising?

(*The four* GROUPS *wake up, stretch and sit up*)

ONE GROUP MEMBER: Red sky at morning, shepherd's warning.

PHAETHON: Up we go – into the clear blue yonder. Up into the powder blue sky printed with vapour footprints. So many footprints! My father drives along this same path every day – over the same towns. You'd think he might vary the route now and then . . . (*Shakes reins*) Hiya! When I take over from Father, I shall follow the Great Circles – drive all over the sky, scaring the birds. This is easy. Lemon squeezy. Tame. It's a hack. It's like riding a haywain home: clippity clop, clippity clop . . .

(*Pretends to fall asleep out of boredom; almost loses balance and steadies himself by putting a hand on the whip*)

Ooo. What's this?

(*Tentatively waves the whip*)

When I take over from Father, there will be a few changes, I can tell you! I shall make some days long and some days short. Sometimes I'll float across the sky like a soap bubble. And sometimes I'll gallop across in half an hour. That'll keep them guessing!

(*The four* GROUPS *kneel to pray*)

I say, that'll keep you guessing! You down there! You don't know it's me, do you? You think it's Helios, my father! There you all are, down on your knees. All praying to *me*.

(*Lets go of the reins to wave the whip tentatively*)

HELIOS: (*as if thinking aloud*) No, Phaethon! Not the whip! Put the whip down!

PHOEBE: (*to herself*) Don't show off, Phaethon. Not now. Just keep your mind on driving!

PHAETHON: Out of my way, birds! Make way for Phoebus!

(*Gets a bird dropping in the eye, staggers, then cracks whip at the bird*)

Urgh! You— Take that!

(*Sound of neighing and galloping hooves.* PHAETHON *lurches into gallop, afraid, then excited*)

Wheeeee!

PHOEBE AND HELIOS: Phaethon, NO!

(PHAETHON *cracks the whip twice more then staggers and drops the whip. Grabbing the sides of the chariot, he rocks wildly from side to side*)

PHAETHON: Oh, help! Oh, whoa!

HELIOS: (*to himself*) Reins. Reins. Pull on the reins, Phaethon.

PHAETHON: Reins. Reins. Pull on the reins.

(*But it is hopeless*)

ARCTIC GROUP: (*sharing the lines*) Higher and higher the chariot rears, taking with it its warmth.
The earth below shivers.

Ponds turn as white as blind men's eyes; the trees as white as an old man's hair. The grass turns to needles.
The air is clogged with the fog of our frozen breath.

PHAETHON: Oh no! Whoa! Whoa back!

DESERT GROUP: (*sharing the lines*) Then down he plunges, the fiery chariot-wheels charring the fields, felling our herds to their knees with their heat.
The ground crazes into jigsaw pieces of brown dirt.
The fruit shrivels on the trees. Our pools shimmer into mirages and are gone. We pant. We thirst. We scorch.
Somewhere, far away, polar ice melts . . .

PHAETHON: Oh, the gods! Daddy! Where are you? Why did you let me . . . ?

SEA GROUP: (*sharing the lines*) Polar meltwater swells the sea.
Wild winds, stampeded by the sudden heat, the sudden cold, roll around the world,

weeding up towns, whipping the sea into raging ranges of mountainous waves.

PANIC GROUP: (*sharing the lines*) What is happening?
Come to our aid, you gods!
The sun is a bubble floating outward into space!
The sun is a meteorite crashing to earth!
See it run helter-skelter around the sky!
Oh, Zeus, Zeus, come to our aid!

(*Enter* ZEUS *from stage right,* CLYMENE, LAMPETIE *and* PHAETHUSA *from stage left*)

ZEUS: Suddenly there is snow on the peak of Olympus. Suddenly shadows sprawl from my feet to all points of the compass.

Helios! What is the meaning of this? (*Startled to see* HELIOS *on the ground*) Helios! Who is driving . . . ?

HELIOS: My son, Phaethon—

CLYMENE: Our son, Phaethon—

PHAETHON: Oh, Mother, Father, help me! The horses won't stop! I can't make them stop! What am I going to do?!

ZEUS: He must be stopped.

HELIOS: The horses will tire. They'll turn for the western stables of their own accord.

CLYMENE: He's a good boy, really! He meant no harm.

SISTERS: Forgive him, Zeus.

ZEUS: There is no time for forgiveness or pity. He is destroying the world! He is ripping up the patchwork planet. I have to stop him.

(*Produces thunderbolt*)

CLYMENE AND SISTERS: NO!

(ZEUS *points the thunderbolt. Sound effect of thunder-clap.* PHAETHON *staggers as if struck*)

PHAETHON: Mummy! Daddy! 'Snot fair, Mummy!

(*He drops down behind chariot front*)

HELIOS: My boy!

ARCTIC GROUP: He is gone like a hailstone in the heat, gone like one of the solar flames that erupt from the sun then disappear. The sun chariot gallops on empty. The horses are winded. They turn for their red stables in the west. Sunset.

HELIOS: Oh, my son. My poor, foolish son.

CLYMENE: The sun has gone out in me for ever.

PHAETHUSA AND LAMPETIE: Oh, Phaethon, why did we let you go? Why didn't Mother and Father say no?

PHOEBE: Oh, Phaethon. My poor, dear brother.

(ZEUS *spreads his arms.* CLYMENE *and the* SISTERS *go to him and he encompasses them in his arms. Exit* ZEUS. *The women are now trees*)

DESERT GROUP: Up on the hill, there are four poplar trees which weren't there before.

SEA GROUP: They toss in the wind like mourners at a funeral.

ARCTIC GROUP: The wind rustling their leaves sounds like weeping.

PANIC GROUP: Amber oozes from their bark in great yellow drops, like golden tears.

ALL GROUPS: (*sharing the lines*) Helios, Charioteer of the Sun, is alone again, without son, without wife or daughters. But he sheds no tears . . . or if he does, they evaporate in the heat of the Sun.

(HELIOS *mounts the chariot and drives*)

Driving his solar chariot, keeping his eyes on the stables of sunset, steering an even path.

Beneath him, the earth bears the scars inflicted by his son – scorched desert, frozen wastes.

Beneath him four poplar trees waving on a hilltop weep amber gum.

But Helios does not look down. He drives at a steady pace and a level height, looking ahead between the ears of his horses.

HELIOS: Trot on. Now. Trot on.

(*Exit* ALL)

Zeus in Love

With such a reputation as a philanderer, how is Zeus to woo and win a wife?

Cast

ZEUS

WINE GIRL

HERMES

DANAE

LEDA

EUROPA

IO

HERA

Costumes

- apron with pockets for Leda

Props

- Zeus's throne
- wine-cup
- stuffed robin, e.g. Christmas tree decoration
- piece of bread
- gold glitter
- white feathers

Idea!

Look at the art which Greek myth has inspired, especially the loves of Zeus and the birth of his children.

Note

You may wish to alter the ending, depending whether the play is being acted in isolation or with others following it.

ZEUS IN LOVE

Alone on stage, ZEUS *sits in his throne, looking majestic. In due course, a* GIRL *enters, bringing him a cup of wine.*

HERMES: (*entering only to corner of stage, as if announcing at a grand ball*) Zeus! Brightness of Sky! Downfall of the Titans! King of the Overworld! Supreme Commander! The Triumphant Conqueror! Thunderer! Earth-Shaker! Sender of Storms! Turner of Seasons! Gatherer of Clouds! King of the Gods.

DANAE: (*entering*) Marvel of marvels!

LEDA: (*entering*) Wonder of wonders!

IO: (*entering*) Matchless Immortal!

HERA: (*entering*) The ultimate husband.

(*All the* LADIES *sigh.* ZEUS, *taking notice of the* GIRL *with the cup, grins, jumps up and starts chasing her hotly*)

HERMES: And an incorrigible womaniser. Zeus could fall in love more easily than a cow falling off a roof. A sweet smile, a flashing eye, a girlish laugh, and he was sunk.

ZEUS: (*breaks off from the chase, panting*) Is it my fault if I have a big heart? It's all in the hunt, you see. It's not the catching so much as the chase. From the top of Olympus I can see all the women in the world, and some of those women – oooh. Cut to the chase!

(WINE GIRL *is chased off stage*)

HERMES: The trouble is, he can't take no for an answer.

The more shy and chaste the girl, the more Zeus wants her. And being a god—

(ZEUS *gives him a frosty look*)

And being *the* god among gods, Zeus has magic enough to break down the stoniest hearts. He lays siege to women.

DANAE: I was locked in a high tower with no door. A soothsayer had told my father that my child would be the death of him. So he locked me into a high tower with no door. I lived a twilight life, encased in rock, like a bulb in an earthenware pot.

ZEUS: So I made myself into gold and twinkled down onto Danae.

(*He goes to stand beside* DANAE, *throwing gold sparkle over her*)

A dazzle of light, a glittering torrent of desire. She caught me in her hands. I fell on her eyelashes, on her mouth, on her breastbone. Gold!

LEDA: I saw no god. I looked up and thought – a swan! There's a swan riding home on the shoulder of evening.

(ZEUS *goes to her and they face each other*. LEDA *pulls from her apron pockets two fistfuls of white feathers which she crams against her head before letting them drop all over her*)

Down he swooped – covered me with his white wings: my eyes and mouth and hands were full of feathers.

EUROPA: A swan I might have fought off. But not a bull. He came to me, flicking flies about with his tail, as I suppose he flicks the stars about with the tip of his finger. I didn't suspect a thing – climbed up on his back and rode him down to the sea.

ZEUS: Down to the sea. Into the sea. Over the sea and

away. What a day! Didn't we find a whole new continent to graze in?

HERMES: My own mother – Maia – though she lives at the far end of deepest night, in a pale sisterhood of virgin stars, twinkled in the corner of Zeus's eye and caught his attention. (*Indicates himself*) Or where would I be, now?

(*He takes out a notebook*)

Four Titans, two sea nymphs, six princesses and a queen, and that's not to mention—

(*Looks right and left and is just about to confide in the audience*)

HERA: *This* is the man who wooed me to be his wife. Me, whose veins flow with Titan blood: this roué, this philanderer, this gigolo.

HERMES: (And her brother, to boot.)

(HERMES *retires to corner of stage*)

HERA: Is this a fit bridegroom for an immortal?

ZEUS: But I could make you Queen of the Gods.

HERA: Queen of the Olympians. The Olympians who wrested Heaven from us Titans and slaughtered my ancestors. Thank you, no!

(She turns her back)

ZEUS: So I made myself small – smaller than my immortal size, smaller even than a mortal. I crammed all my ardour and majesty and eloquence and magic into a— *(parting his hands to reveal a stuffed robin)* a robin. And I hopped on to Hera's windowsill.

(ZEUS goes and stands alongside HERA, robin held up on the palm of one hand)

HERA: Ah! A dear little robin! And so tame!

(She takes it onto her own hand)

See how it sits in the palm of my hand! Lets me stroke him.

ZEUS: *(wriggling with the pleasure of being stroked; to audience)* See how my breast glows red with the heat of my passion.

HERA: Won't a itty-bitty robin sing to Hera, den?

(ZEUS whistles tunelessly)

Who's a pretty boy, den?

ZEUS: Oooo!

(Unseen, he hides a large lump of bread in his mouth)

HERA: Here, birdy. Have a crumb of bread.

(ZEUS spits out the bread disgustedly. HERA makes kissy noises at the robin. ZEUS takes it out of her hand, tosses it

over his shoulder and gives her a passionate embrace.
HERA *is too stunned to object*)

HERMES: They say the hills broke out in flowers on the wedding day – thrust up pansies and jonquils and forget-me-nots and campion and yellow archangel to make a bed for the King and Queen of the Gods.

ZEUS: I made her Queen of Heaven, you see, and (*ultra romantic*) Queen of my heart.

HERA: (*shrill, wagging a finger*) And if I ever see you so much as smile at another woman, you will wish your father had eaten you, along with your brothers and sisters.

(*Exit* HERA)

ZEUS: (*calling after her*) Would I, my love?

HERMES: Well, would he? Naturally, now no pretty face had any power to stir Zeus. He was impervious. Never tempted. From that day on, he led a life as sober and chaste and virtuous as . . . as . . . as . . . *as if*!

(*The* WINE GIRL *slinks across the stage;* ZEUS *sees her and goes cantering after her lecherously; she spots him and runs. He chases her off stage*)

The Kidnapped Bride

Deep in his dark and dismal kingdom, Pluto wanted a wife. But he really should have asked before helping himself to one.

Cast

DEMETER

PERSEPHONE

PLUTO

3 GHOSTS

ZEUS

HERMES

RIVER (unseen, in front of stage)

Costumes

- the gods as elsewhere
- leafy headgear and cloak for Demeter
- circlet of flowers for Persephone
- grey gauzy scarves for ghosts

Props

- throne with sparkling black drapes
- posy of flowers
- plate
- handful of dry leaves

Special Effects

- three spotlights and black-out

Idea!

Choose (or create) music to convey the brightness and colour of the upper world and then the bleakness and gloomy depth of the Underworld.

THE KIDNAPPED BRIDE

Three spotlights pick out and isolate PLUTO, PERSEPHONE *(centre) and* DEMETER. PLUTO *sits in a throne draped in sparkling black.* PERSEPHONE *holds a posy of flowers.* RIVER *is stationed out of sight in front of the stage (where he/she can catch the thrown posy).*

PLUTO: I'm gloomy. I know: it's my place to be gloomy. Gloom is my place. Gloomy Pluto, god of the gloomy Underworld. But was it so unreasonable? To crave company? Warmth? *Light.*

DEMETER: (*only worried as yet*) I only turned my back for an instant, and she was gone – disappeared. Nowhere to be found. Persephone? Don't run off now!

PERSEPHONE: It was the primroses. I saw them and I just wanted . . . It was the primroses.

PLUTO: That's what she was to me. A primrose. I went to the mouth of my subterranean kingdom, and I glimpsed her – up there in the sunlight. So bright. So alive. So . . . gladdening. I was tempted. I admit it.

PERSEPHONE: A sudden blast of cold. The sound of horses' hooves behind me. Then someone grabbed me by the hair!

(PLUTO *grabs her and pulls her into his spotlight. Their two spots join, if possible; if not, her spotlight goes out*)

DEMETER: (*scared*) Persephone? Persephone? Where are you, child?

(*General lighting increases to a workable level but spotlight remains bright on* DEMETER)

PLUTO: (*offering his throne*) I didn't mean to frighten you. Please. Sit down, won't you? I mean you no harm.

PERSEPHONE: No! I have to get back to my mother. She'll be looking for me. What is this place? It's so dark.

DEMETER: Persephone? Don't go hiding now! You're frightening me!

PLUTO: This is Hades. The Realm of the Dead . . .

(*Enter 3 silent, white-faced* GHOSTS *wearing gauzy scarves*)

Oh, don't worry about them. They're always curious to see a new face. You'll have a bite to eat, won't you? A glass of wine?

PERSEPHONE: I'm not hungry. Please let me go. What do you want with me? I don't like it here.

DEMETER: Look for her, trees! Search for her, rivers! Find my little girl!

PLUTO: You could be queen of all this, you know. The Underworld is bigger than the Upper World. There are more souls down here than up there.

PERSEPHONE: Ghosts, you mean?!

(Tosses posy over front of stage)

Quick! River! Carry this to my mother and tell her where I am!

(PERSEPHONE *cowers back in her seat*)

DEMETER: Breezes! Brooks! Look everywhere! I'm out of my mind with worry.

PLUTO: That was foolish. Why did you do that? You shouldn't have done that.

PERSEPHONE: Let me go! I want to go home!

(From in front of stage RIVER *tosses the flowers to* DEMETER)

RIVER: (*unseen*) Demeter! Your daughter is in Hades! Pluto has stolen her away for a bride!

DEMETER: No!

PLUTO: Please. Have an olive? Or a boiled egg? (*Aside*) (If I can just persuade her to accept my food, she is mine, by all the laws of hospitality!)

DEMETER: (*dragging* ZEUS *out of the wings and into her spotlight*) Zeus! Brother Zeus! Come quickly and tell him! Tell Pluto! Tell him to give her back!

ZEUS: What? Who? Calmly, sister! Who's upset you? Tell me. Calmly.

PLUTO: A mushroom, perhaps? Or a truffle? We grow the very best, down here in the dark.

GHOST 1: Who is she, master? She's very beautiful. Dazzling. She almost hurts our eyes.

(*The other* GHOSTS *murmur agreement and shield their eyes while shuffling forward to pluck at* PERSEPHONE)

PLUTO: Yes, yes. Keep back, then. Don't crowd her. This is Persephone. She is not quite used to our low-lighting just yet. Give her time. When we are married, she—

PERSEPHONE: Married! Oh no! Mother! Mother, where are you? I want to go home!

DEMETER: So what are you going to do about it? Command Pluto to give her back! Quickly! I can't bear to think of her down there in that dark with *him*.

ZEUS: Ah now, Demeter, let's try to see both sides of this. Pluto deserves a little happiness, doesn't he? I know there's a certain difference in their ages, but I don't see why, given time—

DEMETER: (*covering his mouth*) Stop! Don't even talk about it! I won't let you! I swear: if you don't make Pluto give me back my daughter, here and now, I'll let the whole world go hang! Do you seriously think I could give my mind to decking the trees . . . or ripening the grain . . . or colouring the flowers . . . or hanging up berries in the bushes . . . knowing my little Persephone was down *there*, with that great dark *abductor*? She's all light and newness! She's all sweetness and promise! Let Pluto smother her in darkness down there? No! Never!

ZEUS: Oh now, sister. You don't mean that.

DEMETER: (*majestic*) Try me! How long do you think your worshippers will go on glorifying you, Zeus, when their vines are shrivelling and the trees are bare and the grass stays underground? How long do you think Mankind will go on honouring you, when the rivers jelly into ice and the clouds rain down tears of hail and sleet? Hurry, man! *Hurry!* Even now he may be mauling my baby with his great paws!

ZEUS: (*duly frightened*) I think you're being hysterical, Demeter. But . . . if it matters so much to you . . . I suppose I must mediate . . . Hermes! I say, Hermes! Come! I have a message for you to carry down below!

(*Enter* HERMES. ZEUS *whispers in his ear. The spotlight shining on* DEMETER *and* ZEUS *goes out*)

PLUTO: A few grapes, my dear? Or a crumb of cheese? A slice of newly baked bread, then? Or a little crispy seaweed? You must eat, child, or you'll fade away to transparency, like these others here.

PERSEPHONE: I— I don't . . . I just want my mother.

PLUTO: Of course. Naturally, I'll send word to her.

PERSEPHONE: You will?

PLUTO: Yes, yes. She'll be here soon . . . but just before she comes . . .

PERSEPHONE: I am very hungry.

(*Starting with the* GHOST *nearest the wings, each speaks then passes a plate to the next* GHOST. GHOST 3 *gives the plate to* PLUTO)

GHOST 1: Little does she realise how
She's thwarted Pluto's plan till now.
She's going to weaken now and eat –
Open her mouth – take in defeat.

GHOST 2: She doesn't know, poor little fool,
Hospitality's binding rule;

How, if she eats, she has accepted
Love she thinks she has rejected.

GHOST 3: But now she'll eat and stay for ever!
Alive and light, and leave us never!
How much brighter things will be,
With shining Queen Persephone!

PLUTO: Here, look. Some pomegranate seeds. Taste.

(*He offers her the plate and she reaches one hand into it.*

HERMES *leaps into the circle of light*)

HERMES: *Stop!* Pluto, you old fox. What are you trying to
do? Trap this child into eating?

PERSEPHONE: (*through a mouthful of food*) Eating? Why
shouldn't I eat?

PLUTO: (*dancing around with glee*) Too late! Too late!
She's mine now! She's eaten! Look! Look! Pomegranate
seeds! A dozen pomegranate seeds!

PERSEPHONE: What? I don't understand. What have I
done? Hermes! Have you come to take me home?

HERMES: I don't know, child. Have you eaten? Did you eat
from that dish?

PERSEPHONE: No. No! I didn't eat anything! Not really!

HERMES: Open your hand, Persephone.

(*He prises open her fingers one by one. The* GHOSTS
gather round to look and HERMES *shoos them away.*
PLUTO, *too, cranes his neck, anxious to see if any are
left in her palm*)

One, two, three, four, five, six. Six pomegranate seeds left
out of a dozen. Not exactly a banquet, but— Pluto, you're a
rogue and a bounder.

PERSEPHONE: No! Why? What has he done? Tell me!

PLUTO: She's mine! She's mine! She's mine! She's mine! From now till eternity! My own little taste of sunlight!

(*All three spotlights again shine on separate spots, to show* DEMETER *and* ZEUS; HERMES; PLUTO *clasping* PERSEPHONE)

DEMETER: Tell him, Zeus! Tell him you forbid it! Reach down below ground brother, and make him give me back my daughter!

ZEUS: She ate his food.

HERMES: Six pomegranate seeds. Not exactly a four-course lunch.

PLUTO: But she ate them!

ZEUS: And all the rules of hospitality clearly state—

DEMETER: (*menacing*) Remember what I said, Zeus. Where will your 'rules' be when I bring back Chaos? Who will ever again be able to offer this *hospitality* you talk about, when every pomegranate has rotted in the fields and the fruit trees have cried themselves naked? Keep my daughter from me, and Nature can strangle itself in bind-weed for all I care. I'll abandon it!

(ZEUS *ponders the problem*)

HERMES: (*to audience*) It's a dilemma, certainly. Mother Nature bereft of her daughter, or Pluto alone and lonely in his gloomy Underworld. How can Zeus decide: for his brother and against his sister, or against Pluto and in favour of Demeter?

PERSEPHONE: (*to* HERMES) You notice no one asks what I want.

HERMES: I noticed that.

ZEUS: I have decided. Let no one question my judgement. Demeter shall have her daughter back—

PLUTO: But—

ZEUS: *For one half of the year!* The world cannot do without Demeter's tender magic – teasing the blossom out of bare boughs – coaxing flowers out of their bulbs, the corn out of the seed. Persephone is her joy and her inspiration. I cannot let Demeter grieve at the world's expense.

PLUTO: And me? I who never get to walk waist deep through a field of corn or wallow in the sea on a hot day – or smell a field of lavender . . . I close my eyes in darkness and wake up to the same darkness! Aren't I to have one little sliver of beauty? One little white hand in my black one? Is it such a crime to fall in love?

PERSEPHONE: Love? You never said anything about Love!

HERMES: Oho! Big mistake, Uncle.

ZEUS: *Zeus is still speaking* . . . in case anybody is interested! For half the year Persephone shall live with her mother in the Upper World. But because she ate half the seeds on the plate, for the other half of the year she shall live with her husband—

(*Gasps of astonishment*)

PLUTO: YES!

ZEUS: . . . She shall live with her husband, I say – with my brother Pluto – in the Halls of the Dead!

DEMETER: Owowow! Do you call that justice?

HERMES: (*leading her aside*) More than most mothers can hope for, surely, after their daughters are married? Be content.

DEMETER: (*pulling away*) I won't! I won't be content!

PERSEPHONE: (*putting her hand into* PLUTO'*s*) I am content, Mother.

DEMETER: But *you* won't be alone! Half the year alone!
Half the year *alone*!

   (*Exit* DEMETER. *A handful of dry leaves falls – from
above if possible*)

GHOST 1: What are these brittle little ghosts, come down
to Hades?

GHOST 2: I never saw a ghost like this before.

GHOST 3: The trees are dying!

HERMES: (*going to look offstage*) No, only crying.
Crying away their leaves;
dropping them onto the breeze.

   (*The* GHOSTS *speak their lines without going to look*)

GHOST 1: The furrowed fields are frowning;
Blackening and browning.

GHOST 2: The brooding sky is scowling –
A chilly north wind howling.

GHOST 3: The sun itself is paling;
The jaundiced clouds prevailing.

GHOST 1: The summer birds are leaving;
The whole of Nature grieving.

HERMES: All Nature is lamenting . . .

PLUTO: . . . But I am unrepenting!
When I give back my lover,
The green world will recover.

   (*Putting an arm round* PERSEPHONE, *he leads her off
stage.* ZEUS *summons* HERMES *with a nod and they exit
together on the other side. Two of the spotlights go out.
The* 3 GHOSTS *huddle together in the last central
puddle of light*)

GHOST 2: (*to audience*) Don't begrudge us, please, our
stolen queen;
She is our candle in this edgeless night.
For us, she is the memory of Green;
To a blind race, the glimmering of light.

GHOST 3: For us she smiles the smile we cannot smile;
Makes for a little, little, little while
The unbearable
Endurable.

GHOST 1: Endure the mud, the slush, the dreary rain,
The dingy days, the bare and leafless tree.
Remember: *you* will soon see Spring again,
When we, The Dead, give back Persephone.

(*The last spotlight goes out*)

What's in a Name?

Both Athena and Poseidon want the new city to be named after them. Fortunately, King Cecrops has thought of the perfect way to settle the argument.

Cast

ZEUS

7 CITIZENS (variable)

ATHENA

POSEIDON

KING CECROPS

2 operators for PANTOMIME HORSE

Props

- throne
- baby
- cut-out silhouette of the Acropolis 74
- tray of olives

Costumes

- gods as elsewhere
- pantomime horse costume
- crown for Cecrops

Special Effects

- drum roll
- thunder clap
- howling winds and crashing waves (optional)

Idea!

Greet your audience with plates of (stoned) olives, pomegranate seeds, grapes, etc., or circulate them during the interval to keep people in the mood.

WHAT'S IN A NAME?

ZEUS's *throne stands extreme right, hiding behind it a tray of (stoned) olives.* ZEUS *is seated in the throne, lost in thought, even when a crowd of* CITIZENS *mill on stage from both sides.* CITIZEN 1 *is holding a baby. Those who speak come alternately from right and left wings.*

CITIZEN 1: What shall we call it? What?

CITIZEN 2: A name's so important, isn't it? So much depends on it!

CITIZEN 3: It must be auspicious.

CITIZEN 4: It has to be acceptable to the gods.

CITIZEN 5: It must be euphonious.

CITIZEN 6: (*boggling at* CITIZEN 5) It must be *pronounce-able.*

CITIZEN 1: So what to call it?

ALL CITIZENS: What to call the new city?

> (*The* CITIZENS *fetch on stage a cut-out flat of the Acropolis with the Parthenon, etc., ranged round it.*
>
> *Enter* POSEIDON *from left*)

POSEIDON: Well naturally they must call it after me: Poseidon, Ruler of the Seas.

> (*Enter* ATHENA *from right*)

ATHENA: After me, you mean, Pallas Athena.

POSEIDON: But it's right next door to the sea. Of course it's mine!

ATHENA: Nonsense! It's four miles inland. Do these people look like fishermen and beachcombers?

POSEIDON: When Corinth was choosing its patron, they chose me sooner than Apollo because my power was 'second only to Zeus's'!

ATHENA: Well you have Corinth, then, and I'll have this one.

POSEIDON: How can they call it after you? You're a . . . a . . . (*seeking the most insulting term*) a *woman*. My own niece, for Elysium's sake! And what kind of name would it have, named after you? Pallas Town. Pallassos.

ATHENA: And if they named it after you, what then? They couldn't even spell it!

CITIZEN 2: Poseidon. I before E except after . . . E before I except after . . .

CITIZEN 3: (*putting her right*) I before E, except in Poseidon.

CITIZEN 4: We should ask Almighty Zeus!

ALL: Yes! We should ask Zeus to decide!

ZEUS: (*rousing, startled*) Who, me?

(*He looks between* ATHENA *hands-on-hips and* POSEI-DON. *A tricky dilemma*)

Ohoohoo. What I say is . . .

In my opinion . . .

My judgement is . . .

. . . I have decided that . . .

(*Enter* KING CECROPS)

(*Seeing a way out*) King Cecrops should decide!

ALL: Ah yes! Of course! The King should decide!

(CECROPS *bows to* ZEUS)

CECROPS: (*with irony*) Your holiness is most kind. MOST kind. Now, let me see. Who should be the patron deity of the new city? To whom should that great gleaming temple yonder be dedicated? To whom should we pay our tributes and make our most sweet-smelling sacrifices? To Poseidon the Storm-Waker, Sea-Quaker, Earthquake Maker? . . . Or to Pallas Athena – grey-eyed virgin sprung from the very forehead of Zeus?

POSEIDON: (*bragging*) I command the watery world! My subjects outnumber the creatures on dry land! I built the walls of Troy with my own hands! I waged war against the Titans!

ATHENA: I taught Mankind the secrets of ploughing and

weaving! My father is the most powerful of the gods; my mother the wisest. In the war against the giants—

CECROPS: Yes, yes, yes. Naturally, I know you are both infinitely worthy of honour. But if I have to choose between you (*looks resentfully at* ZEUS) (as I must, apparently), I have to put my people's interests first. I have to ask myself: what could you, sir, or you, lady, DO FOR THEM? . . . There now! The perfect solution! It has just come to me! I shall name this infant city of ours after the one who gives her the finest *christening gift*!

ALL CITIZENS: (*variously*) Yes! / Yeah! / Great idea! / The best gift, yes! / Fantastic! / Good old Cecrops! / Why didn't we think of that?

ZEUS: (*aside*) I wish I'd thought of that.

(*Exit* ZEUS, *vacating his throne.* CECROPS *sits down in it. The* CITIZENS *sit around his feet.* POSEIDON *and* ATHENA *are taken aback, then recover themselves and ponder.* POSEIDON *is first to think of something*)

POSEIDON: Aha, yes! I have the gift to end all gifts! Wait here! Don't go away!

CITIZEN 1: What will he bring us?

CITIZEN 2: Walls like he built at Troy?

CITIZEN 3: Jewels from the bottom of the sea?

CITIZEN 4: Salt, maybe, to flavour our food!

CITIZEN 5: Or the four winds in a leather bag – for when our merchants set sail.

CITIZEN 6: It's so exciting!

CITIZEN 7: A present from the God of the Sea!

(*Re-enter* POSEIDON *holding a rope, its end still off-stage*)

POSEIDON: People of Poseidon City! I bring you a gift to make you the envy of every city state and nation. It will make you unconquerable in battle! In peacetime the equal of every creature in creation. From the rolling combers of my ocean; born in the churning cauldron where all Life began . . . I give you:

(*Drum roll*)

THE HORSE!

(*Enter saggy* PANTOMIME HORSE. CITIZENS *gasp and fall back in wonder*)

CITIZENS: (*variously*) Oh wonderful! / What a marvellous animal! / It's like the ones that pull the sun chariot! / Almost. / It must have lots of uses. / Can you eat it? / The horse!

(POSEIDON *looks smug and triumphant*)

CECROPS: Lord Poseidon, you honour us with your gift. It is truly . . . magnificent . . . But now it's the turn of Pallas Athena.

CITIZEN 1: How can Athena come up with anything better than that?

CITIZEN 3: She's already given us the plough and the secret of weaving.

CITIZEN 5: We feel like gods – choosing which is best of two presents!

ATHENA: (*goes and puts something into* CECROPS*'s hand*) I give you this.

CITIZEN 7 : It's not very big, whatever it is.

(CECROPS *looks quizzical. What to do with it? 'Eat it,' mimes* ATHENA. *He eats it and looks pleased*)

ATHENA: I give you a gift to transform your lives. I give

you . . . THE OLIVE. Eat it, yes, or crush the blood from its little body to fuel your lamps, cook your food, smooth your skin, oil your axles, shine your hair . . . Olive trees ask little water and the thinnest soil. And when the sun blazes at midday, you can sit in the shade of your olive trees and drink a cup of wine to this city of yours – this city of mine: to Athens!

(ATHENA *produces a tray of olives and the* CITIZENS *rush to taste them, then descend from the stage in a hubbub of delight, passing through the audience, doling out olives*)

CECROPS: It would seem the people have chosen. Goddess Athena – gracious virgin – my kingdom thanks you for your gift. The temple on the Acropolis will be dedicated to you. Once a year we shall stage a great festival in your honour. Lord Poseidon, what can I say . . . ?

(*Sound effects (optional) of howling winds, crashing seas, seagulls, excluding thunder.* POSEIDON *is raging*)

POSEIDON: Say? *Say?!* Save your breath for swimming, Cecrops! I offer you a horse and you settle for a . . . a . . . PIP! Well, I'm away to my blue-roofed palace, to muster my sea monsters and stampede my brass-hoofed horses. I shall send a tidal wave twenty fathoms high to DROWN your puny city! I'll poison your fields with salt and fill up your wells with rotting fish! I'll drive my sea chariot through your palace and root up every flower and bush and OLIVE TREE *in the entire kingdom*!!

(*Clap of thunder. Enter* ZEUS *in full splendour*)

ZEUS: NO, BROTHER POSEIDON! I FORBID IT. I, Zeus, father of the gods, give the city to my daughter Athena. Swallow your pride, unruly man, as you swallow ships, as you swallow the rivers, as you swallowed Atlantis. Leave your horse and go. Corinth is your city. Let Athens be sacred to my daughter for ever more!

(POSEIDON *gives a great roar of temper and frustration and leaves. Exit* ZEUS. CECROPS *breathes a sigh of relief, takes off his crown, wipes his brow, slithers down in his throne with his eyes shut. The* HORSE *goes over and nudges* CECROPS, *making him jump. He pats the* HORSE)

CECROPS: Here. Have an olive.

(*The* HORSE *shudders and backs off*)

Ah. Don't like olives, eh? Well then . . . We shall have to see who can be persuaded to grant us the everlasting gift of sugar lumps, shan't we?

(HORSE *nods vigorously and they exit together, chatting*)

Love and the Blacksmith

When the ugly blacksmith god asks for the hand of Aphrodite, no one takes him seriously. But to Hephaestus, love is no laughing matter.

Cast

HEPHAESTUS

5 CYCLOPS, blackened hands and faces

APHRODITE

ZEUS

HERA

HERMES

POSEIDON

ARES

Costumes

- gods as elsewhere
- Hephaestus dirtier; Velcro on chest to hold flower in place
- single large eye for each Cyclops, to be stuck on the forehead

Props

- The Chair (Zeus's throne with added decoration?)
- artificial gold leaves on bendy wire (as sold at Christmas) attached to arms of The Chair
- lightning bolt in the shape of a heart
- carnation with Velcro attached
- 2 pairs bicycle clips

Special Effects

- smoke canister under chair (optional, but very effective!)
- pre-recorded blacksmithing noises – hammering, clanging metal, etc.

Idea!

In stories beauty nearly always signifies goodness while ugliness signifies wickedness. Not here. To the Greeks, the Cyclops were an 'alien race'. Find ways for them to move and talk that will imply they are likeable aliens.

LOVE AND THE BLACKSMITH

The CYCLOPS *stand stage left, miming the work of black-smiths, to the sound of pre-recorded clanging and hammering. Each has one big eye stuck to their forehead and is twisted or lame or awkward-looking, knees bent, elbows sticking out, etc. Their nature is very gentle, their speech childlike, and they agree with everything* HEPHAESTUS *says.* HEPHAESTUS *is clearly fond of them.*

(HEPHAESTUS *somersaults on stage right. The* CY-CLOPS *rush to help him up and dust him down, sympathetic and caring*)

HEPHAESTUS: (*shouts off and upwards*) Unnatural woman! What kind of mother throws her own son out of the window?

CYCLOPS 1: And such a high window, too!

CYCLOPS 2: The window of Heaven!

CYCLOPS 3: Just for being ugly!

HEPHAESTUS: All day I fell – the sky shrinking above me, the Earth rushing up to meet me: screaming for the gods to stretch out a hand and catch me. Like a snail thrown down by a thrush to smash it. I broke. Look at me. I was ugly before. Now I'm like a lump of pig iron, burned black by the forges.

CYCLOPS 4: Good job you landed here.

HEPHAESTUS: In the world's smithy.

CYCLOPS 5: Where we can look after you.

HEPHAESTUS: (*tousling* CYCLOPS 4*'s hair*) Yes. Good job I fell here. She only bore me to get back at her husband, you know? Zeus fathered Athena without her help, so Hera says: 'Two can play at that game!' . . . Except that Athena was born out of love, and I was born out of spite. These things show in a child. Athena was everything you would expect in a goddess: beautiful, witty, accomplished. Me, I was ugly, clumsy, squat. Still: I was her son. You'd think she might have loved me a little. But no. She never loved me. (*Shouts, off and upward*) You never loved me!

ALL CYCLOPS: We love you, Hephaestus!

HEPHAESTUS: Yes, yes. I know. My kindred spirits. You Cyclops prised me off the floor and took me in. You showed me nothing but kindness.

CYCLOPS 5: You teach us how to make beautiful things!

HEPHAESTUS: (*cheering up, hugging them*) And we do, don't we? Here in the volcanoes we make tools fit for the gods.

CYCLOPS 1: Cannot manage without us!

CYCLOPS 2: We make breastplate for Athena!

CYCLOPS 3: Arrows for Artemis!

CYCLOPS 4: Cups for Dionysus!

CYCLOPS 5: Chariot wheels for Helios!

CYCLOPS 1: Thunderbolts for Zeus – KERBOOOM!

> (*They all make kerboom noises and roll about on the floor laughing, wagging their legs in delight*)

CYCLOPS 2: (*sobering up*) Hephaestus makes the loveliest things.

CYCLOPS 3: Trident of Poseidon.

CYCLOPS 4: Palace on Olympus.

HEPHAESTUS: Oh yes. I am allowed back onto the mountain whenever I choose. The Olympians need their blacksmith god. I make them things of beauty, and the gods *love* beauty, don't they?

(*Enter* APHRODITE *upstage right, a memory only, holding pose of a dumb blonde*)

That's why they all loved Aphrodite. (*Softer, slower, choked voice, clearly besotted*) Oh, Aphrodite.
One day she just . . . *condensed* out of seafoam.
The essence of beauty. The loveliest woman a god could conceive.
I loved her instantly: more than breath or light or life.

ALL CYCLOPS: (*raucous, laughing*) So did everybody!

(*Exit all but* APHRODITE *who stands examining her nails.*

Enter ZEUS *and* HERA, *she bristling with temper, suppressing her jealousy*)

HERA: It's quite absurd! I mean Ares's tongue is practically dragging on the ground. Hermes is standing there with his feathers steaming. Poseidon keeps showing his muscles and threatening to fight people. Aphrodite is causing mayhem. DO something, Zeus.

ZEUS: Yes. Even poor old Hephaestus is lovesick. Look at the last thunderbolt he made me.

(*Holds up heart-shaped thunderbolt*)

But what to do? If I marry her to one, the others will seethe with envy. We might even have a war on our hands!

HERA: Then don't let her marry anyone! (*Pleased with her own idea*) That's it! You must forbid Aphrodite to marry at all. Well? Artemis has forsworn men.

ZEUS: Yes, but in her case the men didn't mind . . .

(*Enter* ARES, HERMES, POSEIDON *busy arguing, pushing each other*)

Very well. No marriage for Aphrodite.

HERA: I don't think they heard you.

ZEUS: (*bellows*) I said, Aphrodite shall never marry.

(HERMES, ARES *and* POSEIDON *jump, stare, then burst into tears on each other's shoulders. Enter* HEPHAESTUS, *dragging the throne awkwardly out of the wings*)

HEPHAESTUS: (*before we see the chair*) I've made something.

(*Gradually everyone's attention is caught as* HEPHAESTUS *drags the chair centre stage*)

A throne for the Queen of Heaven. A present for my esteemed mother.

HERMES: It's magnificent!

POSEIDON: Fantastic!

ZEUS: Amazing. Hephaestus, you have surpassed yourself, boy!

HERMES: (*to audience*) Poor Heifer. Still trying to buy his way back into his mother's heart. That's quite a present.

HERA: A throne? For me? How . . . gratifying. I have always thought . . . something like this . . . in keeping with my rank. Is it comfortable?

HEPHAESTUS: Try it, please! It's my very best work. I have never taken such pains over anything. Please. Be seated, Mother.

(HERA *sits, wriggling pleasurably, looking regal. Last of*

all, she rests her hands on the arm rests, through the ornate 'cuffs')

Comfy?

HERA: Mmmm. For metal, it is surprisingly warm.

(HEPHAESTUS *passes in front of throne and discreetly folds shut the cuffs.* HERA *struggles*)

Heifer? It's got hold of me. What's happening?

ZEUS: Heifer?

HEPHAESTUS: I have come to ask a favour.

HERA: Tell it to let go, Heifer!

ZEUS: (*amused*) Is this supposed to be funny, Heifer?

HEPHAESTUS: (*still friendly*) The thing is . . . I know you have said no one is to marry Aphrodite, but I thought: if she were to marry me—

(Explosive grunts from all sides, then laughter.
HEPHAESTUS *waits patiently)*

If Aphrodite were to marry me, there would be no war in
Heaven . . . Well, not with me being the armourer of the
gods. Eh?

HERA: Stop blathering, goblin, and get me out of this chair!

HEPHAESTUS: I'm afraid I can't do that.

ARES: Hephaestus marry Aphrodite? Ha ha! That's a good
one.

POSEIDON: Beauty and the Beast, eh? Ha ha ha!

ARES: Princess and the Frog. That's priceless, that is!

ZEUS: Is this some kind of a practical joke, Heifer?

HEPHAESTUS: I was never more serious in my life.

(He crosses to APHRODITE *and goes to touch her face.*
She pulls away. He stares at her, transfixed)

I loved her the very moment I saw her. Perfection made
flesh. She is everything the soul cries for from the moment it
exists, long before it has words to express its longing.

HERMES: *(brotherly, concerned)* She's just a woman,
Hephaestus.

HEPHAESTUS: I knew then, in that instant, I would do
anything to have her for my wife.

HERA: Something's happening! I'm getting very warm.
Zeus, tell him to free me.

ZEUS: Hephaestus, free your mother.

HEPHAESTUS: No.

(General shock and astonishment)

Not until I am married to Aphrodite.

HERA: Ooo! Ow! The chair is getting hot! This chair of yours is getting hotter!

HEPHAESTUS: You should feel the heat of the furnaces down in Sicily, where the Cyclops work making trinkets for the gods.

HERA: Well this is quite warm enough for me, thank you. Get me out.

HEPHAESTUS: First give me Aphrodite for a bride. I'm your son, aren't I? It's time you were finding me a bride.

HERA: You? Marry Aphrodite? Don't be ridiculous. You're . . . you're . . . you're a . . . a . . .

HEPHAESTUS: Reject? Yes. Imperfect goods? Seconds? I know. But I can love as much as any man and more.

HERA: Heifer! The seat! It's getting hotter every moment!

HEPHAESTUS: My name is *not* Heifer. I am Hephaestus, God of the Forges. God of the Volcanoes. Armourer to the Gods. Master of the Cyclops. Son of Hera.

HERA: Hephaestus! I want to stand up!

ZEUS: (*amused, despite himself*) Hephaestus, this has gone far enough. Let your mother out.

(HEPHAESTUS *slowly and deliberately gets out carnation and sticks it to his chest, back turned on his mother*)

HERA: (*whispering*) I smell smoke!

HERMES: (*aside*) Was there ever such a wooing?

HERA: Zeus! Tell him he can have her!

ZEUS: Ooo now, I don't know, my dear. You distinctly said—

HERA: (*to* HEPHAESTUS) You can have her! Take her! She's yours!

APHRODITE: Oh, now come on! Don't I have any say in this?

HERA: No!

APHRODITE: But I don't want to marry him. Look at him. I'd be a laughing stock, married to the ugliest lout in Heaven!

HERA: Be quiet, you stupid girl, and plight him your troth!

APHRODITE: My what?

(*Smoke billows out from under the chair*)

EVERYONE BUT APHRODITE: YOUR TROTH!

(APHRODITE *bursts into grizzling tears.* ZEUS *drags her and* HEPHAESTUS *together by the wrists and claps their hands together*)

ZEUS: I now pronounce you god and wife. You may kiss the bride.

APHRODITE: No he may not!

(HERA *is freed and goes fussing loudly off stage, taking everyone with her but* HEPHAESTUS *and* APHRODITE, *who face each other across the width of the stage*)

They can't make me kiss you.

HEPHAESTUS: (*sadly accepting*) No.

APHRODITE: Or care one fig about you.

HEPHAESTUS: I know.

APHRODITE: I won't be faithful to you, you know?

HEPHAESTUS: I don't suppose you will . . . You should

warn your lovers, though. I am very jealous and very . . . (*indicates the chair*) *inventive*.

APHRODITE: Hate is all you can expect from me. Night and day. Hate.

HEPHAESTUS: I know. But at least you will have me in your head. You can't hate someone without thinking about them.

APHRODITE: You ridiculous buffoon. I'll love whoever I choose! You can't stop me!

> (*Exit* APHRODITE. HEPHAESTUS, *left alone, takes the carnation off his chest and looks at it sadly. Enter the* CYCLOPS *shyly, gauchely*)

CYCLOPS 1: How did it go, Master?

HEPHAESTUS: Oh! Fine. Fine. Everything went just to plan.

CYCLOPS 2: Is the wedding over?

CYCLOPS 3: Did we miss it?

HEPHAESTUS: Yes, yes, I'm sorry.

> (*They look around for the bride*)

The bride . . . she had to go. Very busy, the Goddess of Love.

CYCLOPS 4: (*disappointed*) We did make a wedding present. For you two.

> (*They give him the gift and he unwraps it*)

HEPHAESTUS: How very kind of you.

CYCLOPS 5: She is very lucky lady, to marry our Master.

HEPHAESTUS: (*holding up 2 pairs of bicycle clips*) Perfect . . . What exactly . . . ?

CYCLOPS 1: Bicycle clips they are. Two pairs.

HEPHAESTUS: Ah! Very useful.

CYCLOPS 2: They will be . . . when bicycles come along.

(HEPHAESTUS *tries on the clips in various places (e.g. ears). The* CYCLOPS *point out his mistake and he puts them on his shins. Shyly the* CYCLOPS *leave.*

HEPHAESTUS *looks at the carnation again. He crosses to the empty chair*)

HEPHAESTUS: This is for you, Mother. I got married today.

(*Sits down and pretends to be* HERA)

Oh, that's lovely, son. How kind. Thank you. She's a lovely girl. I hope you'll both be very happy.

(*Stands up again, as himself*)

Thank you, Mother. I'm sure we will. I'm sure we will.

(*Places carnation on seat of chair, mimes kissing* HERA's *hand, then walks off stage*)

Weaving Magic

Arachne's weaving is the most beautiful anywhere. Her big mistake is in proving it.

Cast

ARACHNE

5 ADMIRERS

ATHENA

at least 3 other GODS (e.g., ZEUS, APOLLO, APHRO-
DITE, HERA)

Costumes

- shawl for Athena
- Arachne's 'spider' costume (see illustration)
- gods as elsewhere

Props

- 2 embroidery frames, one portable, containing piece of
embroidery or tapestry
- a whistle for Zeus to wear round his neck
- 5 yellow dusters
- rectangle of (maybe) holographic card, to be torn up at
each performance

Special Effects

- clap of thunder (or waffle board)

Idea!

The original myth ends with Arachne hanging herself and Athena saving her by changing the rope into a cobweb and Arachne into a spider. How could this ending change how the audience feels towards the two women? How are you going to make your audience like the heroine and hate the villain?

WEAVING MAGIC

A huddle of women stand blocking our view of ARACHNE, *who sits at her embroidery frame. Balanced on the frame is her 'competition piece' – holographic card, maybe, or a repro classical masterpiece. The cries of the women suggest they are admiring a baby.*

ADMIRER 1: Oh, Arachne, how beautiful!

ADMIRER 2: Perfect in every tiny detail!

ADMIRER 3: Even down to the little fingernails!

ADMIRER 4: How I do envy you, Arachne.

ADMIRER 5: Such a gift!

(*Enter* ATHENA *disguised as an old woman with a shawl over her head*)

ATHENA: What is all the excitement about?

ADMIRER 5: (*breaking away from crowd*) Oh it's Arachne's latest! Wonderful! Just gorgeous!

ATHENA: A boy or a girl?

ADMIRER 5: (*puzzled, then laughing*) Oh bless you, love, it's not a baby. It's an embroidery! She's finished another of her embroideries! There's no one to match her with a needle. The woman's not made who can sew or weave better than Arachne.

(*The crowd breaks up.* ARACHNE *can be seen now, though the frame has its back to the audience*)

ATHENA: Let me see. (*Looking at the embroidery*) Hmmm. That is a very great gift the gods have given you.

ARACHNE: Ooo, I don't know about that. I wasn't born embroidering, you know. I just worked at it, year in, year out. My mother taught me most of what I know. I worked out the rest myself.

ATHENA: But the Muses must have blessed your handi-work.

ARACHNE: I didn't know there was a Muse of embroidery.

ATHENA: And there is the goddess Athena to be honoured, of course. Patroness of the arts and crafts. She is the greatest embroiderer on Olympus. You should pay honour to her for your talent.

ADMIRER 1: I bet she isn't as good as Arachne.

ATHENA: (*stiffening with rage*) *She isn't what?* (*Recovering herself*) What would you say to that, Arachne? Would you say that your work was better than that of the goddess Athena?

ARACHNE: I'd say . . . I never met Athena, nor saw any of her work. All told, I expect I'm as good as her, if not better.

(*Crack of thunder*)

ATHENA: PROVE IT!

(*She sheds her disguise. The five* ADMIRERS *fall to their knees whispering 'Athena!', 'It's Athena!'* ARACHNE *stays standing, head proudly erect*)

A contest! To see which of us is the greater artist! Alas, arrogant Arachne, you should not have pitted yourself against the gods. What mortal ever outdid the gods? At least . . . what mortal ever did so and WON?

ARACHNE: (*coolly*) What mortals were ever given the chance? Thread your needle, madam, and let's put the matter to the test. I am game.

(*A piece of sewing is brought to* ATHENA)

ADMIRER 1: Oo, Arachne, is this wise?

ADMIRER 2: To compete against a goddess?

ADMIRER 3: What if you should lose?

ADMIRER 4: (*aside*) What if she should win?

(*Enter other* GODS, *en bloc:* ZEUS, APOLLO, APHRO-
DITE, HERA, *or as desired. They stay in a tightly packed
huddle all the while they are onstage*)

GODS: What odds, what odds
Will you lay on the gods?
And who dares to back the
Mere mortal Arachne . . . ?

ZEUS: Not me!

HERA: See how they sit, side by side,

Weaving pictures nine spans wide;
As through the threads their needles glide

APHRODITE: . . . both oooozing pride.

ADMIRER 1: Like a fall of hair, the threads stream from Athena's fingers: like a waterfall.

> (*Some use could be made here of coloured lighting, if available*)

ADMIRER 2: Wonderful! A picture of animals and birds . . .

ADMIRER 3: Colours as bright as reef fish.

ADMIRER 4: Stitches as small as seeds.

ADMIRERS 1, 2, 3, 4: Masterly!

ADMIRER 5: Arachne, though, uses every colour of the rainbow and more besides: she dyes the threads herself.

ADMIRER 4: And her stitches are small as grains of sand.

ADMIRER 3: (*anxious, to herself*) Oh, Arachne. Shouldn't you *pretend* less skill than you have?

> (ZEUS *blows a whistle*)

ADMIRERS: Time's up! Time's out. The competition is finished!

GODS: Who can doubt the outcome?

ATHENA: Let us see now who is the finer needlewoman!

ADMIRERS: Who is going to judge?

GODS: Who is going to choose?

ADMIRERS: Who is going to win?

GODS: And who is going to LOSE?

ATHENA: (*gliding to centre of stage, taking command*) I shall choose, of course. Who else? Am I not the goddess of weavers and seamstresses? Am I not the patroness of every useful and elegant art ever entrusted to the puny peoples of Earth? *See the picture I have woven!*

(*She holds up her piece of tapestry to everybody on stage. Last of all, she shows* ARACHNE)

ARACHNE: It is lovely, madam, anyone can see that.

ATHENA: (*looking smugly triumphant*) I think you will agree that I have no choice but to award the prize to myself as—

ARACHNE: But you have still to see mine.

(*She shows her picture (stiff paper) to those onstage without the audience being able to see it. They gasp with amazement*)

ADMIRER 1: (*to audience, coldly*) It is ravishing.

ADMIRER 2: It is past description.

ADMIRER 3: The very figures seem to be alive – on the verge of moving.

ADMIRER 4: And what has Arachne chosen to weave?

GODS: (*stuffily shocked*) The gods on Olympus!

ADMIRER 5: (*trying to suppress a laugh*) Swaggering and preening themselves and falling out of Heaven . . .

ADMIRER 1: (*joining in the laughter*) . . . cheating and bleating and quarrelling and caterwauling . . .

ADMIRERS 2, 3, 4: (*hilarious*) As foolish and mulish as anyone on Earth!

(*The* GODS *huff and puff and stalk off stage, still bunched up in a body. The mortals continue to laugh until* ATHENA *holds up her hands for silence*)

ATHENA: (*brittle, teeth set in a grin, badly disguised ill-grace*) Aha, a masterpiece! I admit it! Quite superb. Beyond anything I could . . . I have ever troubled to make. Credit where it's due. The work is flawless. Perfect. The prize must be yours, Arachne, ha ha ha. Too good for words . . . And so *very* true to life . . .

> (*Going to* ARACHNE *as if to shake her hand, she snatches the 'embroidery' and rips it in shreds. The other women drop down in terrified awe.* ARACHNE *is also on her hands and knees trying to gather up the pieces when* ATHENA *towers over her and 'pecks' a furious hand at her clothing, appearing to pinch her but in fact releasing the ties around her arms – see illustration*)

For your craftsmanship, I award you the laurel wreath! May you go on beautifying the world every day of your life! . . . And for *lampooning the gods* may the world reward you (*shrieking like a fishwife*) by tearing down your work each time they see it! Live long, Arachne! Weave and drape your tapestries in every dark corner of every home in the world! They shall be your hammock to sleep in, your nets for catching food. And everyone who sees them will wince with disgust and sweep you away, you and your children and your children's children's teeming children!

> (ARACHNE *stands up, arms out. The* ADMIRERS *recoil in disgust*)

ADMIRER 1: Ergh. What is it? So black and so gross?

ADMIRER 2: What is it, with its waving, crouching basket-work of legs?

ADMIRER 3: A spider!

ADMIRERS 4 AND 5: (*clutching each other*) A spider?!

ATHENA: A spider. The first of *billions*. (*Points into audience*) Let that teach you, NEVER to do ANYTHING better than the gods who made you! Do you hear? Do you?

> (ATHENA *storms off. The* ADMIRERS *pull yellow dusters from their pockets and begin to flick at* ARACHNE)

ADMIRER 1: Get out! Get out, you filthy creature!

ADMIRER 2: Dirtying my nice house.

ADMIRER 3: Creeping and crawling. Urgch!

> (ARACHNE *scuttles here and there and finally runs off stage with a great cry*)

For the Sake of Love

Life without Eurydice is unbearable. That's why
Orpheus is ready to follow her into the realms of
the Dead.

Cast

HERMES (optional)

ORPHEUS

EURYDICE

3 FANS of Orpheus's music

CHARON, the ferryman

CERBERUS the guard-dog (3 people)

the DEAD (at least 4)

PLUTO, God of the Underworld

Costumes

- grey scarves for the Dead and Charon
- 3 dog masks for Cerberus (available from party shops)
- shawl for Eurydice
- black clothes, highwayman's mask (and hat?) for Charon
- Pluto as elsewhere
- cloak for Orpheus

Props

- small lyre for Orpheus
- an oar for Charon

Special Effects

- pre-recordings of echo-effect words, running water, bird-song, a jangling discord, something sublime for Orpheus to 'play', a) happy, b) heartbroken, c) sleepy, d) 'desolate' chords

Ideas!

Listen to some of Gluck's *Orpheus and Eurydice*.

Talk about how this scene could be lit, whether or not lighting equipment is available.

FOR THE SAKE OF LOVE

Ideally, bright lighting at first, then reduced lighting to represent the Underworld. Birdsong (recorded or produced on a 'warbler') implies a sunny summer day. HERMES *enters upon an empty stage.*

HERMES: Do you like love stories? Do you understand about love? You must. You're alive, after all. Everything and everyone living understands about love. Even the Dead, come to think of it.

(*Enter* EURYDICE, *stage right*)

Eurydice. In love up to her ears.

(*Enter* ORPHEUS, *stage left*)

Orpheus. In love up to his ears.

(*Bright, bright lighting.* ORPHEUS *plays his lyre. Pre-recorded music or sensuous sound effect*)

EURYDICE: Oh, Orpheus! I don't deserve you! The finest musician in the whole world . . . and my dearest love. Even the animals are spellbound by your music.

ORPHEUS: Oh, Eurydice! You are every note of music I play.

(*They approach each other, hands extended*)

EURYDICE: How lucky we are to have found each other!

(*She snatches at her ankle in pain. A snake has bitten her*)

Ow! My ankle! A snake! Orpheus! Oh, Orpheus!

ORPHEUS: No!

(EURYDICE *sinks down.* ORPHEUS *runs to her. Jarring discordant blast of notes. Enter 2 of the* DEAD *who escort* EURYDICE *away. He catches hold of her shawl as if to restrain her, but they exit, leaving the shawl in* ORPHEUS*'s hands. He speaks to it as if it were her body*)

No! No! She's not dead. She can't be dead! Not my girl! Not Eurydice! Eurydice! Open your eyes! Eurydice! I can't live without you . . . Eurydice!

(*Echoing sound effect.*

Enter crowd of FANS)

FAN 1: Sorry to hear your news, Orpheus.

FAN 2: Play your lyre, it will make you feel better.

FAN 3: Yes, play for us, Orpheus. Play us a tune!

FAN 2: Something pretty.

FAN 1: People get over these things.

FAN 2: Time is a great healer.

FAN 3: We have to accept the will of the gods.

ORPHEUS: No!

FAN 1: What? You won't play?

ORPHEUS: I won't accept the will of the gods! I don't accept the will of the gods! I can't!

(*The* FANS *close in oppressively near, to comfort him, saying soothing things. He breaks violently free*)

I can't live without Eurydice. I refuse to live without her! I'll go to the Underworld and fetch her back!

(*General consternation*)

FAN 1: He's gone mad with grief, poor soul.

FAN 2: Does he mean he's going to kill himself?

FAN 3: No one goes to the Underworld before they are dead. It's not possible!

ORPHEUS: Pluto! You hear me, Pluto? Make her no bed among the shadows. Set no place for her at your table! Hold off your clammy hands! Don't sprinkle decay on her face. I'm coming to fetch her back! (*Runs off*)

FAN 1: What a waste. The world's greatest musician, going to his death.

FAN 2: Nah! He'll never get the ferryman to row him over.

FAN 3: Even if he did, Cerberus the guard dog would tear him in pieces.

FAN 2: When did Pluto ever let the living enter Hell?

FAN 1: Enter, maybe. But leave again?

ALL FANS: NEVER.

(*Exit* FANS. *Enter* CHARON *to stand stage left, bored by routine. Sound effect of flowing water. Dimmed lighting, stage left. Enter* ORPHEUS, *stage left*)

CHARON: Hail, traveller. Open your mouth. (*Peers into* ORPHEUS's *mouth*) Where's the coin? Where's your fare? Did you die at sea? Or don't you have any friends and family to give you a decent burial? (*Touches him and pushes him away*) What's this? You're not spirit! Get away with you. This is no place for the living!

ORPHEUS: I have to cross over.

CHARON: Most are more eager to stay on this side.

ORPHEUS: (*gets out money*) Here. You wanted a coin? Here are coins. Have them. Take them all. I have to cross over.

CHARON: (*refusing the money*) Ah! I see. A child, was it? Someone dear to you? Someone you cared about? It happens. Don't worry. Time heals. Time is a great healer.

(*Makes as if to go.* ORPHEUS *gets out lyre and plays.* CHARON *turns back, shines a torch at* ORPHEUS)

You are Orpheus the musician. All my passengers talk about you. Look! The water has stopped flowing to listen! Even the ghost carp are gaping up at you. You have a gift like that, and you want to die?

ORPHEUS: No! But without Eurydice I can't live. I can't play! *She* was the gift the gods gave me – not music! If you had a wife like Eurydice, you could make music like mine!

CHARON: Get in. I'll row you over. You may catch a glimpse of her from the boat. It's the best I can do. But you'll never get ashore. Pluto has set Cerberus to keep the likes of you out of the Underworld, and no one gets past Cerberus alive.

ORPHEUS: Let me deal with Cerberus.

CHARON: No one deals with Cerberus.

(*As they 'row', the whole stage grows darker. Enter* CERBERUS *stage right –* 3 PEOPLE, *feet together, arms round each other's neck. One howls, one growls, one barks. They paw the air*)

Don't you know anything, you poor fool? Cerberus has three heads, and in each head, three rows of teeth. Cerberus is a great slavering hulk of sinew and rage, kept always starving, always kennelled in darkness, always in pain. The banks of the Styx are gouged hollow by his scrabbling claws. (*Jabs his oar at the dog*) . . . Get back, you brute!

ORPHEUS: Even he was a puppy once.

(*He begins to play. One by one, the heads of* CERBERUS *are pacified by the music. The heads look at each other, sway along with the tune.* ORPHEUS *tickles them under their chins)*

Good boy. Who's a good boy. Sit. Down. Poor beast. Stay till I come back.

(*Exit* ORPHEUS *stage right*)

CHARON: How can he do otherwise, Orpheus? Is he not chained in the darkness? No one leaves their place here in Hades. Their darkness goes on for ever.

(*Exit* CERBERUS. CHARON *retires to edge of stage.*

Enter the DEAD, *like the* WWI *picture 'Gassed', but wearing grey gauzy scarves)*

THE DEAD: Welcome to Sheol,
Welcome to Hell,
Welcome to Tartarus, the bottomless well.
Welcome to Hades,
Welcome to Dark,
Welcome to Pluto's flowerless park.
Welcome to eternal, sad Oblivion.
Not for us the joys of sweet Elysium.

(*Enter* ORPHEUS, *calling* EURYDICE's *name*)

Here we drift, through clammy dark,
An army of souls assembling;
Speaking our names through bloodless lips;
Whispering, remembering.

(ORPHEUS *searches among them for* EURYDICE)

We prisoners here are tightly crammed,
Head to fleshless head we stand,
Boneless hand in gauzy hand,
Populating Pluto's land,
While the rocks break down to sand;
We wistful, whispering, weary band.

(ORPHEUS *begins to play his lyre. The* DEAD *are drawn towards him, into a moving circle, facing outwards, hands reaching, appealing to the audience*)

Pay the ferryman his due;
Pay Charon his penny;
You happy, happy, happy few,
Remember us, we beg of you:
We are what you are coming to,
We wistful, wishful many . . .

DEAD 1: What is that sound? I remember it! I half remember . . .

DEAD 2: . . . like a perfume . . .

DEAD 3: . . . like a dream. It's music! But here, in the Underworld?

(*Enter* PLUTO, *raging*)

PLUTO: What's happening? What current is flowing through my domain? My subjects are all drifting like water towards a drain— (*Seeing* ORPHEUS) What?! An interloper? A living soul?

(ORPHEUS *kneels. The* DEAD *fall back to the rear of the stage, cowering*)

ORPHEUS: I have come for Eurydice. For my wife. There was a mistake. She came here too soon.

PLUTO: I never make mistakes. Nor does my servant, Death. Death never makes mistakes. Seize him, spirits, and peel his body from his soul. (*Makes as if to go*)

ORPHEUS: But you do, mighty Pluto! You have done! In taking my Eurydice, you mistakenly turned the world upside down. Now all the Upper World is plunged into darkness. And all of Hades is choking on light.

(PLUTO *looks upwards*)

Give me back my wife, your Highness. Give me back my Eurydice and I shall sing songs about you that will make men long to die, simply to be in your presence.

PLUTO: Ah! I see. One of the broken-hearted. For that, I pardon you. Well, I don't know how you got in here, but if you go now, my ferryman Charon will row you back to the other side. Cheer up. Time is a great healer.

ORPHEUS: But your Honour! Your holiness! . . . Each springtime *you* lose your own wife – Persephone – lovely Persephone! Each springtime, you lend her back to the Upper World for half a year. But what if it weren't a loan – if you had no prospect of seeing her again . . . if, when she went, she was gone for ever, could *you* go on living? Could *you* draw breath? Could *you* lift the lids of your eyes to look out, or put your heart to the pain of beating? Would Time heal *your* grief? Give me back Eurydice, or I shall rattle your black gates for the rest of my sorry life.

PLUTO: Stop! Enough! How dare you liken your mortal feelings to mine? Not another word!

ORPHEUS: No more words, then. Only music. Only the sound of a man's heart breaking into minims and breves.

(*He plays, reducing everyone to tears*)

DEAD 1: It's sadder than the eagles plucking at Prometheus.

DEAD 2: Sadder than Sorrow climbing out of Pandora's box.

DEAD 3: Sadder than Daedalus mourning for Icarus.

PLUTO: (*looking up*) Oh, Persephone, where are you? I miss you so much while you're gone . . . This man . . . STOP! Stop, I said. I don't want you here. I won't have you here. Your music is . . . *subversive*.

(*Thinks for a moment, then smiles to himself and calls offstage*)

Eurydice!

(*The* DEAD *pass the name in whispers*)

Come, Eurydice, wife of Orpheus! Your husband has come to take you home. (*To* ORPHEUS) Take her . . . But you go on ahead. I shall command her to follow in your footsteps.

ORPHEUS: Oh almighty Pluto, I—

PLUTO: But! Don't look back. Do you understand? You must not look at your wife's face until you are standing on the far shore of the River Styx. If you do . . . I shall reclaim her.

DEAD 1: Quickly, Orpheus, hide your eyes, Eurydice is coming!

DEAD 2: Quickly, Orpheus, look away, Eurydice comes running!

DEAD 3: Quickly, Orpheus – on your way! Don't look back, for her sake!

ALL DEAD: For our sake!

(ORPHEUS *turns away just in time not to see* EURYDICE *enter. The* DEAD *space themselves across the stage and* ORPHEUS *and* EURYDICE *weave between them, as if walking through Hades*)

ORPHEUS: I hear the tread of her little feet behind me! Oh, my Eurydice!

ALL DEAD: Our thoughts rise with them, like bubbles rising through wine.

ORPHEUS: Are you there, Eurydice? Keep close! Don't lose sight of me!

ALL DEAD: If she escapes, it is as if we, too, have been given a second chance!

ORPHEUS: Eurydice? Why doesn't she answer? Is she really there? Is it really her?

ALL DEAD: Go on, Orpheus! Don't look back! Trust her, Orpheus! She would follow you to the moon and back!

ORPHEUS: Maybe Pluto is tricking me – punishing me for my impertinence. Perhaps he sent some demon to patter along behind me. Perhaps it isn't her at all.

(*Enter* CERBERUS)

ALL DEAD: Nearly there, Orpheus!
See the great dog Cerberus sleeping by the river?
See the boatman Charon? See the water shiver?

(*The* DEAD *drop back to rear stage right*)

ORPHEUS: Cast off, boatman! Make ready to row! Didn't I say I'd bring her? Be quick! Cast off . . . But don't go without her! Why don't you speak? Is she there? Is it her, boatman? Has she got into the boat? Is my wife in the boat with us?

CHARON: It's not for me to say, sir.

ORPHEUS: Eurydice! Is it you? Are you there? Speak, why don't you? Is it really . . .

(*He looks round.* CHARON *gathers up* EURYDICE *and drags her across stage and off*)

ALL DEAD AND ORPHEUS: NO!

(*Echo effect on 'no'. The* DEAD *troop off, despairingly.* ORPHEUS *freezes, hands in his hair.*

Enter FANS)

FAN 1: Play for us, Orpheus.

FAN 2: Play us something jolly!

FAN 3: Yes! Don't be so *gloomy* all the time. You'll turn the wine sour!

FAN 1: Play us a song, Orpheus! We're on our way to a wedding.

(ORPHEUS *plays a few desolate chords*)

FAN 2: Said a wedding, not a funeral!

FAN 3: Misery!

FAN 2: Killjoy!

FAN 1: Gloom merchant! What's the matter with you these days?

(*They start to slap, punch and kick him. He falls to the ground. The action freezes. Enter* EURYDICE. *She crosses to* ORPHEUS *and extricates him from under his cloak, which the* FANS *now go on maltreating. Draws him away to other side of stage*)

EURYDICE: Come, Orpheus.

ORPHEUS: Where? To the Underworld?

EURYDICE: No. Word came from Olympus. I heard it ricochet through Hades. It dazzled the ears of the Dead. 'Eurydice to the Elysian Fields.' 'Orpheus and Eurydice, to the Fields of Elysium.' Come on, my love. Don't look back. They're not worth it. None of it is. Not worth so much as a backward glance.

(*Exit* ORPHEUS *and* EURYDICE)

HERMES: It's a place reserved for lovers. The Fields of Elysium. A place for lovers and heroes. Its rooftops stand on stalks of light, in meadows of rainbow flowers. It is the place you dream of in your sweetest dreams . . . And there's music now – music in Elysium. Thanks to Orpheus and Eurydice.

(*Exit* ALL)

Echo–Echo–Echo

Echo always wants the last word . . . until Hera
speaks her sentence.

Cast

HERA

3 HANDMAIDS (nymphs)

ECHO

NARCISSUS

Costumes

- Hera as elsewhere
- Narcissus could wear a blond wig to show he is a 'heart-throb'

Props

- pond (optional)
- bench
- largish dictionary
- toy sheep (optional)
- bunch of artificial narcissi
- pot in which to 'plant' them

Special Effects

- At the end, an eerie echo effect can be achieved with a 'Zube Tube'. This can also be banged sharply when the curse is spoken, as it produces unearthly noises.

Idea!

There are lots of other 'origin' stories where natural phenomena are explained by means of myth: e.g., why thunder arrives after lightning; the first rainbow; the waxing of the moon; the shape of the constellations; the seasons.

ECHO–ECHO–ECHO

There is a pool (or suggestion of a pool) mid-stage left, hiding a bunch of narcissi and pot of earth. On opposite side of stage stands a bench, dictionary hidden behind it. There is no one onstage.

(*Enter* HERA *patently near the end of a long, involved joke, followed by her* HANDMAIDS, *including* ECHO)

HERA: So the augurer says to the chicken: 'Don't you want to know what the future holds in store?' And the chicken says—

ECHO: 'Not till they invent Tarot cards!'

HERA: (*annoyed*) Echo!

ECHO: What?

HERA: Hold your tongue, girl.

ECHO: (*silly giggle*) Oops. Sorry.

HANDMAID 1: You were going to tell us about Leto again, Divine Hera – how you wouldn't let her give birth.

HERA: What? Oh, yes. Very well. That husband of mine – so very *generous* with his favours – left that *object* Leto expecting twins. Twins! I ask you. Well, I simply forbad it. Go where you like, I told her. Wait nine months or wait ninety. I have forbidden everyone everywhere and every day of the year to grant you the time or place to give birth. Carry your twins (*milking the story*) through all eternity, because I will never let them see the light of day! And that's what you call—

ECHO: . . . being left holding the baby! Ha ha ha!

HERA: Echo! How dare you interrupt me when I am talking!

ECHO: I didn't, I just . . .

HERA: Well of course you did. Every time I open my mouth, you interrupt me.

ECHO: Didn't.

HERA: Did.

ECHO: Didn't.

HERA: Did.

ECHO: Didn't.

HERA: SILENCE!

(*She waits a long time to test* ECHO's *obedience, then turns away, thinking she has won at last*)

ECHO: Didn't.

HERA: (*in full cry*) Right! Have it your way, Echo! Since you must always have the last word, you shall have it always. The last word and no other!

ECHO: But I was only saying . . .

HERA: Hold her, nymphs, and open her mouth!

(*The* HANDMAIDS *pin* ECHO *down along the bench so that her head is in profile, mouth open.* HERA *reaches her entire arm down, as if into* ECHO's *mouth, but in reality behind the bench, and pulls out the dictionary*)

I confiscate it, your entire dictionary of words! From henceforth you shall have none but those that drop from another mouth, already used, already spoken. Speak your last word, Echo!

ECHO: Oh! Oh!

HERA: Let last words be your only words for ever and for ever!

ECHO: Forever? Forever!

(*Exit* HERA)

HANDMAID 2: At least she won't bore us any more with talking about Narcissus.

HANDMAID 3: (*mimicking*) 'Oh, Narcissus the Shepherd! Narcissus is so handsome! Narcissus is so wonderful! Narcissus is the most perfect man . . .'

HANDMAID 1: She's not wrong, of course. Narcissus!

(*All the* HANDMAIDS *utter a huge sigh and leave. But they are back almost at once, crowding round* NARCISSUS, *who holds a token sheep. They and* ECHO *follow him about the stage mooningly*)

NARCISSUS: Not now, girls! Another time. I'm appallingly busy! . . . Oh well, if I must, I must . . . Hermione, you may wash my clothes this week. Phaedra, you can cut my hair. Asberta, you can cook supper for me on Tuesday – and you on Wednesday – and you on Thursday. Ah! How tiring it is being pursued for one's company . . . (*Sits down*) Ah yes: my little Echo. Now let me see how you can help me . . .

ECHO: Help me! Help me!

NARCISSUS: What say you sing me a song?

ECHO: A song? A song?

(*The other* HANDMAIDS *drift off chattering*)

NARCISSUS: Yes. Sing to me.

ECHO: (*sings*) me-me-me-me-me!

NARCISSUS: What are you doing? Tuning up?

ECHO: (*shaking her head, dragging him to his feet*) Up! Up!

NARCISSUS: Not now, Echo. Not now!

ECHO: Now! Now!

NARCISSUS: What is this, Echo? A joke?

ECHO: A joke. A joke.

NARCISSUS: Well, it's not very funny. Not like you to be at a loss for words.

ECHO: (*achingly*) Words! Words!

NARCISSUS: (*aside to audience*) If you ask me, I think she's gone mad with love.

ECHO: Love! Love!

NARCISSUS: Uhuh. So you want me to love you. Yes?

ECHO: Yes! Yes!

NARCISSUS: (*encouraging her to come closer, as if for a kiss, then . . .*) What, a gauche, dreary girl like you? Don't make me laugh.

ECHO: Laugh? Laugh?

NARCISSUS: Oh, go away.

ECHO: Away? Away?

NARCISSUS: Yes, away. You heard me. Leave me alone.

(*Exit* NARCISSUS)

ECHO: Alone. Alone!

(*Exit* ECHO *following* NARCISSUS.

They re-enter almost immediately, but a passage of time is indicated by a change in ECHO. *Her face is darkly shadowed, bedraggled hair dusted with white*)

NARCISSUS: Oh, this tedious woman! Day after day she trails after me. Week after week she follows me round like a sheep – making sheep's eyes at me, bleating my own words back at me, grinning and grizzling and pulling faces. They're all the same, these girls. No conversation. I mean, kissing is all very well, but now and then a man wants to *talk*! About sport, say. The Olympic Games!

ECHO: Olympic Games! Olympic Games!

NARCISSUS: Ah! You're interested in sport, are you? You amaze me.

ECHO: You amaze me. You amaze me.

NARCISSUS: Here we go again. I really am going to have to be cruel to be kind.

ECHO: Be kind. Be kind!

NARCISSUS: Look, I know you love me . . .

ECHO: Love me . . . love me!

NARCISSUS: But the thing is . . . (*teasing again; then really cruel*) . . . you bore me. You give me a pain . . .

ECHO: (*clutching her heart, ill*) A pain! A pain!

NARCISSUS: . . . here.

ECHO: (*begging him to listen*) Hear! Hear!

NARCISSUS: Endlessly repeating—

ECHO: – repeating, repeating –

NARCISSUS: —what I say.

ECHO: I say . . . I say . . . I say . . .

(*He waits to see what she is about to say, but when nothing comes out he walks away in disgust*)

NARCISSUS: Oh DROP DEAD!

(ECHO *crams both hands against her mouth so as to stop herself repeating these words. He appears to be leaving but comes back at once*)

I'll say this just once, and I want you to listen.

ECHO: Listen! Listen!

NARCISSUS: Do you really suppose a man of my . . . a man like me – Narcissus the Shepherd, Narcissus the Beautiful, Narcissus the most handsome man in the province, is going to choose *you* of all the nymphs I could have? I mean, you're not even pretty any more! You're all rags and bones these days. White face. Hollow eyes. Think again, my dear. Think again.

ECHO: Think again! Think again.

NARCISSUS: (*as if to an idiot*) Your – love – is – in – vain.

ECHO: (*sudden realisation that she has wasted her love on a vain, arrogant pig*) Vain. Vain!

NARCISSUS: You'll just have to wait your turn.

ECHO: (*resolving to be revenged*) Your turn. *Your* turn.

NARCISSUS: Honestly! You girls can be nothing short of a curse.

ECHO: (*pointing at him*) A curse. A curse.

NARCISSUS: Look at you!

(ECHO *changes demeanour; all sweetness again. She takes him by the hand and coaxes him over to the pool*)

ECHO: Look at YOU. Look at YOU!

NARCISSUS: (*caught unawares, confused*) In the pool?

ECHO: The pool. The pool.

NARCISSUS: (*the merest glance*) Mmmm.

(*He steps away, then does a double-take and goes back to look. Take time over this speech*)

Good heavens. Is that me? I am rather . . . Well, yes. I can see why you were smitten, poor girl. I am rather . . . In fact I don't think I ever realised how . . . That face! That hair! That strong aquiline nose . . . Those high cheekbones! That broad brow. Those eyes. There's something so . . . *noble* in that face. I could sit here and gaze at it for ever . . .

ECHO: (*spite and loathing*) For ever. For ever. (*Coughs frailly and crawls off stage weeping*)

NARCISSUS: That manly jaw! That neck . . . That mouth . . . Those lips . . .

(*He bends down to kiss but disturbs the reflection*)

Oh no! Don't go! Don't! Hold still, Narcissus, hold still. The ripples will settle. There. There he is again. Narcissus the Shepherd. Narcissus the Beautiful. My Narcissus. Love of my life . . .

(After a few moments, enter HERA *and* HANDMAIDS *in a closely bunched crowd, masking* NARCISSUS *so that he can slip off stage leaving behind a bunch of narcissi where he sat)*

HERA: I am sorry now that I was so hard on her. I never thought I would say it, but Olympus is too quiet now Echo's gone. I was harsh. I see that. Dear little Echo. See if you can find her, nymphs.

(They spread out to search the stage. Each calls 'Echo!' and is answered with an 'Echo! Echo!')

HANDMAID 1: We can hear her, but we can't see her.

HANDMAID 2: I think she must have pined away.

HANDMAID 3: Left nothing behind but her voice.

HANDMAID 2: It's odd. The pretty shepherd has disappeared as well. No one has seen him for a month.

HERA: Oh look. What a charming flower! I never saw one like that before.

(They cross to the pool and examine the narcissi)

HANDMAID 1: See how it leans over the pool – just as if it's admiring itself in the water.

HANDMAID 3: Vain little flower!

HERA: No, no. Fortunately only the Human Race is guilty of vanity. I can't think why. They hardly compare with these little flowers, do they? . . . Come on. Let's try further up the valley. Echo! Echo! Where are you? Echo!

(Exit ALL*)*

ECHO: *(from off)* *ECHO! ECHO! ECHO!*

The War of the Sexes

A relatively clean version of the notorious play
Lysistrata.

Cast

CHORUS MALE

CHORUS FEMALE

LYSISTRATA

CLEONICE

LAMPITO

MIRRINE

LARA

WIDOW

COMMANDER

5 other SOLDIERS

Costumes

• long tunics for women, short ones for men. *Note to single-sex casts*: If all tunics are dress-length, they can be hitched up or allowed to hang long depending on whether the character is male or female.

Props

• sword
• spear
• saucepan
• baby
• 2 CHORUS labels to be worn round neck

Idea!

Do male and female *still* feel differently about war and fighting?

THE WAR OF THE SEXES

The women – LYSISTRATA, CLEONICE, LAMPITO, MIRR- INE, LARA, WIDOW *– sit about, using the laps of their dresses as embroidery cloth and miming sewing. A spear and sword lean against the back wall.* CHORUS MALE *and* CHORUS FEMALE *take up their positions at the front of the stage looking portentous but for the CHORUS placards hung round their necks.*

CHORUS MALE: (*grandiose*) Many the glorious battle bravely won!
Many the daring deed in battle done.
Many the wounds brought home by men unbowed!
Many the laurel wreaths upon their brows!

CHORUS FEMALE: Empty our broad Athenian streets of men!
And why, you ask? They're off to war again!
The foes may differ, yes, but not the fight.
Their wives, neglected, beg for sweet respite.

(*Gradually the forward-facing oratorion turns to a personal row between the two*)

CHORUS MALE: But men must fight and women (bless their hearts)
Must stay at home and practise wifely arts.
War is a fearful thing, but staunchly we,
The men of Athens, strive for victory!

CHORUS FEMALE: Stony the ground whereon their wives' words fall,
For these great brutes the sword and shield are all.

And so we women yearn unsatisfied
For *sense* to take the place of stubborn pride!

(*Exit* CHORUSES *arguing and jostling*)

GRUFF VOICE OFFSTAGE: Where's me shirt?

CLEONICE: Men!

(*She gets up and goes briefly off stage, returning to take
up her sewing again*)

GRUFF VOICE OFFSTAGE: Where's me sword?

LAMPITO: Always fighting.

(*She gets up and goes briefly off stage, returning to take
up her sewing again*)

GRUFF VOICE OFFSTAGE: Where's me 'elmet?

MIRRINE: Either they're just home from the war, or they're
just leaving for the next one.

(*She gets up and goes briefly off stage, returning to take
up her sewing again*)

GRUFF CLIPPED VOICE OFFSTAGE: Where are my sandals, what?

(LYSISTRATA *sighs, gets up and goes off stage briefly,
then returns to sewing*)

LARA: Part-time husbands, that's what we have.

LAMPITO: Part husband is what I've got! Each time he
comes home something else is missing – an ear, a finger, an
eye. He's left more of him strewn around the battlefields
than he's brought home to me.

WIDOW: Some of them don't come home at all.

LYSISTRATA: That's true. The city is full of widows.

GRUFF VOICE OFFSTAGE: Where's me ... thin-gummy ... whatsit?

LYSISTRATA: (*Gets up and takes the spear off stage, saying as she returns*) Wouldn't you do *anything* to see the back of this war?

CLEONICE: The eyes out of my head.

LARA: Ten years of my life!

LAMPITO: All the food off my table.

WIDOW: Every penny I have in the world. Who are they fighting at the moment anyway? I forget.

LYSISTRATA: What difference does it make? One war is just like every other.

CLEONICE: They got us by false pretences, you know. They did! I married a husband, not an empty space in the bed. Here we are, left to do all the work – tend the farm, run the stall, paint the shutters ...

LAMPITO: I expect they think they are doing us a favour ... you know: saving the world for Democracy and Freedom.

LYSISTRATA: If the world was a democracy, we women would not have to put up with these part-time husbands.

GRUFF VOICE OFFSTAGE: Where's me son?

MIRRINE: (*jumping up and running off stage pleading*) Our son? Oh no! You're surely not taking our boy? He's only a child! Please! Not the boy!

(*She returns weeping*)

LYSISTRATA: We don't have to put up with it.

CLEONICE: What?

LYSISTRATA: We don't! We can put a stop to their never-ending fighting.

WIDOW: Oho, yes.

LYSISTRATA: (*standing up. They gradually realise she is serious*) It's not as if we have no *leverage*. For years they have made us manage without them. Well? It's time our men had to do without *us*! Listen! (*She whispers her plan*)

MIRRINE: Oooh. I don't know about that.

CLEONICE: Maybe the war's not so bad after all.

LAMPITO: Yes. What's so marvellous about peace?

LARA: You can't miss what you've never had.

LYSISTRATA: Listen to you! Is that all the resolve you can muster? Wouldn't it be worth it for a lasting peace? Where's your courage? Where's your moral fibre? Don't we owe it to ourselves? Don't you owe it to your *children*?

CLEONICE: Oh all right, Lysistrata. Tell us what we have to do.

LYSISTRATA: I shall write to the women of Boeotia and Laconia and tell them what we are doing.

MIRRINE: Write to the enemy?

LYSISTRATA: They are women: that makes them our natural allies . . . An oath. We must swear an oath! Let us swear on this sword!

LARA: Is that right? Can you swear an oath to peace on a sword?

LYSISTRATA: You have a point. What shall we swear on, then?

WIDOW: The entrails of a white horse? That's supposed to be good.

ALL WOMEN: Yurgh. Messy.

MIRRINE: (*dreamily*) We could all cut ourselves and let our blood mingle.

ALL WOMEN: Ooowch.

LYSISTRATA: What about a jug of blood-red wine, then!

ALL WOMEN: (*variously*) Mmm! I'll swear on that! / That's more like it. / Good idea! / Wonderful.

(*Exit the* WOMEN)

GRUFF VOICE OFFSTAGE: Where's my little wifey, then? Just time for a little kiss and cuddle before I have to . . .

(*Enter* SOLDIER 1, *expecting to find the women*)

Where . . . ? Uh?

(*Exit* SOLDIER 1. *Short pause, then re-enters with* COMMANDER)

COMMANDER: (*clipped huntin'-shootin' delivery*) The Temple of Athena, eh? Jolly good. Praying for our safe return, eh what?

SOLDIER 1: Not exactly, sir. They've shut and barred the doors against us. They won't let us in to perform our battle rites.

COMMANDER: What are you telling me? We have siege conditions here?

SOLDIER 1: Ceyx went there and they slammed the door on his hand.

COMMANDER: (*defiant and aggressive*) Huh! Huh! (*then just plain bewildered*) Why exactly?

SOLDIER 1: They say they won't come out until we cancel the war.

COMMANDER: CANCEL THE WAR!? Huh! Huh!

(Enter 3 other SOLDIERS, *pointing back off stage as if just come from the temple)*

SOLDIER 2: My Lampito says she won't cook dinner for me!

SOLDIER 3: My Mirrine says she won't feed the chickens if I go . . .

SOLDIER 4: My little Lara says she won't come home – and we've only been married a fortnight!

*(*SOLDIER 5 *comes on awkwardly carrying a baby, looks as if he's about to speak but doesn't)*

COMMANDER: Who's behind all this? Who has been stirring up the ladies?

(The SOLDIERS *look awkward and turn away, whistling)*

Well?

SOLDIER 1: It was your . . . er . . . the Lady Lysistrata's idea.

COMMANDER: My wife! Huh! Huh! Well, then. We shall soon put a stop to this. Form rank!

(The men form rank and space themselves out in crisp military style, then bundle messily after the COMMANDER *who exits stage left. The* WOMEN *enter from right and sit about looking nervous (except* LYSISTRATA*). Re-enter* MEN *from left and stop short so as to call across the stage)*

COMMANDER: Ahem! I say! You there! Ladies! A word if you please.

LYSISTRATA: As many as you like. Words are free.

COMMANDER: What is occurring here, Lysistrata? Let's have you home now, old girl. Quick sharp.

LYSISTRATA: (*hands on hips, defiant*) Not until we have your word that there will be no more wars.

COMMANDER: Oh, is it that old tune again? You really must stop trying to meddle in things that don't concern you. War is man's business.

LYSISTRATA: In the past, yes. But now we are making it ours. All these years we have sat mildly by, watching you come and go, fighting the Boeotians, invading Laconia . . . playing your war games—

COMMANDER: We were defending Democracy and the integrity of the State!

LYSISTRATA: Brawling, you mean. And we were left to tend the farms, train the slaves, mend the roofs, sell the produce . . . and sew up your wounds and praise your heroism each time you came home.

COMMANDER: Huh! Herumph. Small sacrifice for Democracy, wouldn't you say?

LYSISTRATA: And were our sons a small sacrifice, too? The ones you took to war and never brought back?

COMMANDER: Oh now. Let's not open up old wounds. Too painful. Too—

LYSISTRATA: And this Democracy of yours. Does it give us women a voice in the Assembly? Do we have a vote or the power of veto?

(*General laughter among* MEN)

Well, now we have found our voices. And we say you shall do without us until the war comes to an end: no wives, no housekeepers, no lovers, no nurses – until the fighting stops once and for all.

COMMANDER: Lysistrata, you are undermining the war effort!

LYSISTRATA: On the contrary. We shall win a lasting peace. The women of Boeotia and Laconia are in complete agreement. They have already signed the accord.

COMMANDER: Huh! Pah! Ahem-hem. We shall discuss this later, Lysistrata. When you have calmed down. (*He tries to take her aside, whispering*) Don't make a spectacle of yourself, woman.

(*But she shakes him off and the* WOMEN *mime closing the big temple doors*)

LYSISTRATA: When you have sworn peace, we will discuss terms. Until then . . . you know where to find us.

SOLDIER 1: They've closed the temple doors!

SOLDIER 2: Now we can't go in and make our victory prayers.

SOLDIER 3: We could smash the doors down.

COMMANDER: Huh. Huh. No need. No need. The silly chickens will come out of their coop soon enough if we just ignore them. Come on, chaps. Form rank. We have a war to prepare for!

(*As before, they form rank briskly, then bundle haphazardly off stage. The one with the baby seems about to speak to audience, but does not.*

The right side of the stage will now be used by the women. CLEONICE *peeps round the 'door'. Enter the* SOLDIERS *in turn, who speak then sit down, ranging themselves around the left-hand side of the stage*)

SOLDIER 1: (*holding saucepan*) How long does kale take to boil?

(*He sets down the saucepan*)

SOLDIER 2: That green mould on the cheese: can you eat it?

SOLDIER 3: The slaves want to know what provisions to buy.

SOLDIER 4: There are rats raiding the chicken house.

(*Enter* SOLDIER 5 *with baby, looking helpless; he fails to speak*)

CLEONICE: (*peeping out round 'door'*) They look very upset.

LYSISTRATA: Good. (*Moving* CLEONICE *aside,* LYSISTRATA *mimes barring the door*)

MIRRINE: They're so helpless without us.

LYSISTRATA: So much the better.

LARA: Poor babies.

LYSISTRATA: We just have to stand our ground.

(*Enter* CHORUS MALE *and* CHORUS FEMALE *to centre stage front*)

CHORUS MALE: Nobly the wrongèd men withstand the slight
Their silly wives inflict upon their might;
Hurt and puzzled and somewhat subdued
That courage earns them such ingratitude.

CHORUS FEMALE: Single-mindedly the sisterhood
Is holding fast to that they know is good.
Arming their tender hearts against the pity
They cannot help but feel for their poor city.

CHORUS MALE: Tender hearts, indeed! They're simply skiving!
Playing trollops when they should be striving.

CHORUS FEMALE: Silly indeed! Let's hear the groan
From all those noble males left on their own.
We'll hammer all your weapons into ploughs—

CHORUS MALE: You'll never do without us, silly cows!

CHORUS FEMALE: (*versifying breaks down*) Just who are you calling a silly cow?

CHORUS MALE: Yes, pardon me, I mustn't insult the livestock . . .

(*They exit scuffling and scrapping*)

SOLDIER 1: We should batter the door down.

SOLDIER 2: We should give them a good beating!

SOLDIER 3: I mean, the gods never meant us to take this lying down! Look at the muscles they gave us!

SOLDIER 4: Most of yours are between your ears.

SOLDIER 3: Want to say that to my fist?

SOLDIER 5: (*still with baby; dismal*) What good would it do us if we did?

SOLDIER 3: Did what?

SOLDIER 5: Broke down the doors. What would it prove?

(SOLDIER 3 *kicks saucepan so that it goes off stage
front right. The* SOLDIERS *freeze*)

CLEONICE: I miss them.

LAMPITO: They might just as well be away at the war.

LYSISTRATA: But if it means they will never go to war
again . . .

MIRRINE: They'll just take it out on us, instead.

LARA: I miss the smell of them fresh from the bath-house.

MIRRINE: Not their feet, though.

LARA: No. Not their feet. But the rest of them.

(*General groan of accord. The* WOMEN *freeze.*
COMMANDER *re-enters and the* SOLDIERS *stir into life*).

SOLDIER 1: I'm starving to death.

SOLDIER 2: I can't *find* anything.

SOLDIER 3: Our slaves have run off. The house is like a
tomb.

SOLDIER 4: It isn't the food I miss.

COMMANDER: No, it's having a clean tunic to put on.

(*He leaves*)

SOLDIER 4: Yes. What is that smell?

(SOLDIER 5 *sniffs the baby and looks pained. The*
WOMEN *stir into life*)

CLEONICE: I've just remembered! I left a fleece drying. I'll
just go home and fetch it in.

LYSISTRATA: Stay where you are.

LAMPITO: I left some dough to rise. It will go all to waste if I don't get back.

LYSISTRATA: What's a lump of dough in comparison with lasting peace?

MIRRINE: I'll just go and check on the baby. I hear there's typhoid around.

LYSISTRATA: You'll do nothing of the kind.

LARA: (*displaying huge stomach*) Oh my goodness! I feel the labour pains coming on. I've got to go and give birth, but I'll be right back.

LYSISTRATA: You weren't even pregnant yesterday!

LARA: I know. Fancy. I'll be back directly.

> (LYSISTRATA *intercepts her and pulls the saucepan from under her dress*)

LYSISTRATA: (*roaring*) You pitiful objects! Is it really so hard to do without a man for longer than a week?

> (*The* WOMEN *look shamefaced*)

Just sit down and hold fast to the Cause.

CLEONICE: It's knowing they're out there. Going to waste.

LYSISTRATA: And will you really spoil everything for the sake of a kiss and a cuddle?

> (*The* WOMEN *look at her and each other; they nod and drift towards the 'door', which they start to unbar. The* MEN *stir and stand up.* LYSISTRATA *holds up a finger. The* WOMEN *put their ears to the 'door'*)

SOLDIER 1: I can't stand it!

SOLDIER 2: I dream of her every night!

SOLDIER 3: I didn't sign on for this.

COMMANDER: Form rank!

(They ignore him)

I have received a communication from the Laconians. Seems morale is at a low ebb.

SOLDIER 4: Poor dogs.

COMMANDER: And the Boeotians are sending an ambassador to discuss terms.

SOLDIER 5: It wears you down, it does. The longing.

COMMANDER: Herumph. Question is. Whether to enter talks.

SOLDIER 2: With the Boeotians?

COMMANDER: With the . . . er . . . herumph . . . females.

ALL SOLDIERS: *Oh yes!*

COMMANDER: *(approaching temple doors)* Pff. Pff. Herumph. Ahem. T-t-t-t-tch. Wife! I say! Lysistrata!

(LYSISTRATA steps 'outside')

We thought you might like a chance to back down.

LYSISTRATA: No. Thank you.

(Turns to go back 'in')

COMMANDER: Wait! We thought you might want to mend bridges.

LYSISTRATA: Mending bridges is a peacetime occupation. We shall mend bridges when you have disbanded the army.

COMMANDER: Disband it? Then the State would be defenceless!

LYSISTRATA: Better than being childless.

COMMANDER: No, no. You don't understand, woman! Boeotia and Laconia would invade!

LYSISTRATA: That is not what I hear from the wives there.

COMMANDER: (*hugely pompous*) But do not let us forget, wife, that Courage and Heroism are man's greatest virtues!

(*She looks him up and down contemptuously*)

(*feebly*) Anyway . . . we *like* fighting.

LYSISTRATA: I believe there are things you all like more.

(*The* WOMEN *emerge and stand looking beautiful, blowing kisses, beckoning. The* MEN *lurch forwards hungrily*)

COMMANDER: All right! Very well!

LYSISTRATA: You'll sign a peace treaty with Laconia?

COMMANDER: Herumph.

LYSISTRATA: And with the Boeotians?

COMMANDER: Owa . . . very well.

LYSISTRATA: (*as brisk as ever*) Good. Come back when it's done.

(*The* WOMEN *skip back 'inside', bar the temple doors and hug each other*)

COMMANDER: Form rank!

(*The* MEN *go to line up but only hang an arm round each other's neck and slouch off disconsolately.*

Enter CHORUS MALE *and* CHORUS FEMALE)

CHORUS MALE: And so the might of man was undermined.
Demoralised, the three states grew resigned
To years of peace without one shred of glory,
And thus ends most unhappily our story.

CHORUS FEMALE: And so the might of women was affirmed
Who, by their patience, war to peace had turned,
Saving their sons and lovers from wars:
And thus ends well the old, old story.

CHORUS MALE: How are you getting home?

CHORUS FEMALE: That's for me to know . . . Usual way.

CHORUS MALE: It's just that I could walk you.

CHORUS FEMALE: Who? You?

CHORUS MALE: Why not? Handsome woman like you. Shouldn't be out alone after dark.

CHORUS FEMALE: (*coy*) Who? Me?

CHORUS MALE: Always thought: bit of all right, that Female Chorus.

CHORUS FEMALE: Get away with you! . . . You're not bad yourself.

(*They hold hands and toddle off together*)

A Heart of Stone

Pygmalion has no time for women. Time for a change of heart.

Cast

3 PORTERS
PYGMALION, King of Cyprus
APHRODITE
GALATEA
PAGE
PRIME MINISTER
GENERAL
STATUES, as desired

Costumes

- gold band crown for Pygmalion
- Aphrodite as elsewhere
- cheesecloth 'shroud' for Galatea

Props

- mallet and chisel
- tall cardboard box (e.g. fridge size), painted white to represent marble block
- tray (optional)
- mask for Aphrodite

Special Effects

- sound of baby crying

Idea!

George Bernard Shaw updated this myth and his play *Pygmalion* was turned into *My Fair Lady*. Try your hand at updating another Greek myth.

A HEART OF STONE

3 PORTERS *struggle on to an empty stage carrying a tall cardboard box, painted white, representing a block of marble (very heavy).*

PORTER 2: (*grunting and puffing*) Where do we put it? The place is full of marble!

PORTER 1: The King is a very enthusiastic sculptor.

PORTER 3: Good, too. Look at all these. (*Moving among imaginary statues*) It's almost like they're alive.

PORTER 1: Oh, yes. He's as good as they come. Centaurs and satyrs, he carves . . . and athletes and archers . . . gods and gargoyles . . . heroes and harpies . . . orange trees and oracles. Things mythical, historical and botanical.

(*As he names each subject a member of the cast gallops on stage and freezes in the likeness of it, until the stage indeed looks full of statues*)

Works in any medium, too. He carves lemons in limestone, birdbaths in soapstone, marvels in marble, putty putti . . . When he carves a horse, people reach for an apple to feed it. When he carves a cat, children reach out to stroke it.

PORTER 2: No nude nymphs, though. I like a nice nude nymph myself.

(*They hustle him aside.* APHRODITE *enters inconspicuously*)

PORTER 3: Don't you say things like that when the King's around. He can't stand 'em.

PORTER 2: What, nudes?

PORTER 3: Nah! Women! Calls 'em a plague and a pestilence.

PORTER 1: No use nor ornament.

PORTER 3: 'A failed prototype for the tree sloth.'

APHRODITE: (*aside*) Does he just?

PORTER 1: Won't have any in the palace.

PORTER 2: The original male chauvinist Pygmalion, eh?

(*Enter* PYGMALION)

PYGMALION: All right, all right. You've delivered it. You can go now. No need to stand around gossiping like a gaggle of women.

(*Exit* PORTERS. STATUES *gallop after them*)

APHRODITE: (*to the audience*) Time, I think, to teach this loveless man a lesson.

PYGMALION: (*admiring marble block*) Excellent. Lovely grain. A bull this time, I think – or the Minotaur, perhaps, wrestling Theseus.

APHRODITE: (*lifting a mask in front of her face*) You haven't heard about the competition, then?

PYGMALION: (*not attending*) Competition?

APHRODITE: The King of Crete is offering a laurel wreath for the best sculpture of a human form.

PYGMALION: Oh, well, in that case, I shall give him Prometheus bound – or Atlas, perhaps, holding up the sky . . .

APHRODITE: Ah, but it has to be a woman. The rules expressly say: a sculpture of a woman.

PYGMALION: (*gives roar of frustration*) Oh, very well. A woman. This once. There has to be a first time for everything. The Medusa, perhaps. Or some Amazon with one breast cut off for the sake of her archery.

APHRODITE: The winner will be the one whose statue is judged the most *beautiful*.

PYGMALION: A waste of good marble.

APHRODITE: (*leaving*) Remember now. She must be beautiful. And hurry! There's not much time before the competition closes!

(*She sits down on the front of the stage. The* PORTERS *'carry' in* GALATEA, *covered in white cheesecloth so as to look like a statue-in-progress, and set her down centre stage. They remove the marble block.*

PYGMALION *mimes carving round the statue.* PAGE *brings in tray.* PYGMALION *breaks off to mime quick bite and drink, all the while looking at the statue*)

PAGE: (*to audience*) The King, my master, worked like a demon. At first there was a lot of muttering about the waste . . .

PYGMALION: Half a ton of best Parian marble! For a female!

PAGE: But somehow his chisel seemed touched with even more genius than usual. A figure emerged from the marble like Aphrodite herself rising from the sea's foam. Each limb, each feature: perfect first time.

PYGMALION: This is going to be my best work ever. The stone melts from under the chisel!

PAGE: It was almost enough to make King Pygmalion believe in the Muses (if it weren't for the Muses being female). (*As* PYGMALION *tackles the head*) The face loomed like a reflection from a steamy mirror – the most beautiful face imaginable.

PYGMALION: I shall carve her lips ajar – as if she were about to speak but thought better of it. Intelligent, but not forever telling what she knows. Big eyes, but downcast . . . modest, not brazen. In fact I shall carve the kind of woman that doesn't exist.

PAGE: By the time she was finished – *it* was finished, I mean – the statue was so lifelike that it seemed one breath away from moving, speaking, looking him in the eye.

(PYGMALION *sinks down and stares at the statue*)

Master, you haven't eaten all day!

PYGMALION: (*eyes always on the statue from now on*) What? Oh. No. I'm not hungry.

PAGE: It's past midnight. May I go to bed, master?

PYGMALION: What? Oh. Yes. Yes, of course. I must go, too. Quite weary. Didn't realise how late . . .

(*Exit* PAGE. PYGMALION *drifts towards the wings but
comes back and sits down in front of statue.*

Enter PAGE, PRIME MINISTER *and* GENERAL)

PAGE: Somehow, though, my master couldn't tear himself
away from his studio. He locked the door and wouldn't let
anyone in. ('*Knocks*') Won't you eat, master? You haven't
had a bite in three days!

PRIME MINISTER: (*calling*) I really must confer with you
about the Kyrenia situation, your Majesty.

GENERAL: I mean, my troops need new sandals, but he
won't even see me to discuss it!

PRIME MINISTER: Is he ill, do you suppose?

PAGE: He will be, if he doesn't eat.

(*These three freeze*)

PYGMALION: Who are you? What corner of my mind did
you come from? How could I invent a beauty I've never
even seen? (*Shakes himself*) This is absurd. A piece of stone!
A few chisel blows. It's ridiculous! What's got into me? Pull
yourself together, Pygmalion. It's just a woman. If she were
real, you wouldn't even . . . Oh. If she were real. If she
were . . .

(*Gently he touches the knee of the statue. He keels over
and lies on his side curled up*)

PRIME MINISTER: Well? What do you suggest?

GENERAL: Well, I mean, if the King really is *mad*— (*The
others start so he whispers the word*) – mad – we have a
constitutional crisis on our hands. We must have a head of
state!

PRIME MINISTER: And there's no heir! Oh, the gods take
mercy on the poor benighted King!

(*Exit* PAGE, GENERAL *and* PRIME MINISTER)

PYGMALION: (*kneeling up*) Oh, you gods, take mercy on a poor benighted man! Take pity on me! Apollo! Zeus! You know about women – the trouble they are! Hermes! Ares! You know what disasters they bring to a man! Take this one. Spirit her away! Somewhere I can't see her! – NO! Don't! (*speaking the name with great difficulty*) Aph–ro–di–te!

(APHRODITE *sits up attentively though he addresses the prayer upwards*)

Humbly, on my knees, I beg you – take this pain out of me! Eros has been making target practice of me! I'm a fish on a line and the hook's through my heart! I can't break free! Give me a wound to show for it! Something I can die of! I can't go on like this: a fool in love with a lump of stone!

APHRODITE: (*facing front*) In love?

PYGMALION: I never knew. I never looked. I shut my ears against women's chatter. Now I'd give anything just to hear those lips speak – see those eyes look back at me! What a fool! What a ten-times fool I am now – in thrall to this . . . to a . . . What's your name?! Who are you?

(*Curls himself up in a ball of misery, arms over his head.* APHRODITE *goes and removes the sheet, kissing* GALATEA *on the cheek*)

GALATEA: (*dazed, confused*) My name? Oh. I'm sorry. I feel a little dizzy. Can't seem to . . . I remember a brightness . . . (*touches her own cheek*) but before that . . . Do forgive me.

(PYGMALION *gradually unfolds and stares*)

I think I must have stepped inside out of the sun. Do forgive me. I hope I didn't disturb you.

PYGMALION: Disturb me?

GALATEA: I see you are a sculptor. I know artists can't bear distractions. I'll get out of your way. I'm so sorry.

PYGMALION: No! Wait! Don't go! (*When she turns back startled*) You . . . your name. You still haven't told me your name.

GALATEA: It's Galatea.

(*Again she makes to go*)

PYGMALION: Wait! Stay! Don't go! Please, Galatea . . . I don't deserve you, I know, but . . . Don't go. *Don't ever go!*

(PYGMALION *and* GALATEA *freeze, he on his knees reaching out towards her.* PAGE *hurries on, followed by* PRIME MINISTER *and* GENERAL)

PAGE: It was amazing! We've no idea where she came from. She couldn't remember—

GENERAL: Wouldn't say, more like—

PRIME MINISTER: A beauty, yes. Undoubtedly. But what's her family? Her rank?

PAGE: Anyway, the first we knew of it, they were getting married!

PRIME MINISTER: The women-hating King Pygmalion was getting married!

PAGE: You could hear jaws hitting the floor all over Cyprus.

GENERAL: Mind you . . .

PAGE/GENERAL/PRIME MINISTER: SOME WOMAN!

(PYGMALION *and* GALATEA *stand as if to receive wedding guests;* PRIME MINISTER *and* GENERAL *go to shake hands, then all except* PAGE *exit chatting, stage right*)

PAGE: (*picking up chisel and mallet*) Now he has cart-loads of flowers delivered to the temple of Aphrodite every day of the week . . . And he hardly has time for his sculpture, what with the sacred rites and composing love songs and writing poetry and this and that and—

(*Burst of baby crying offstage.* PAGE *gives pained look and runs off*)

. . . the other!

Wish-a-Wish

Be careful what you wish: your wish may come
true.

Cast

SILENUS, a drunken satyr

MIDAS

HERMES

2 SERVANTS

PRINCE (as small as possible)

QUEEN

Costumes

- 2 Phrygian caps for Midas, one multicoloured, one gold; gold jewellery; donkey ears (see illustration)
- horns for Silenus (optional)
- gold band crowns for Queen and Prince

Props

- stone painted gold on one side
- bunch of grapes, gold on one side
- gold (bronze) cutlery
- gold plate
- bucket of finely shredded white paper (water)
- golden covered chocolate coins

Special Effects

- chime bars – the player must be able to see the action
- cow bells
- cymbals

Idea!

Build a 'prop wall' on either side of the stage, with hooks and pockets to hold all the various props needed. Appoint someone to be in charge, changing the props on the wall and checking that they are all available.

WISH-A-WISH

HERMES, SERVANTS 1 *and* 2 *and* PRINCE *sit along the front of the stage.* SILENUS *sits propped drunkenly against the back wall. On the stage is a stone painted gold on one side, gold side hidden.*

HERMES: (*to audience*) There once was a king of Phrygia—

SERVANT 1: Oo, I like limericks. Go on.

HERMES: It's not a limerick, it's a fable. (*Discomposed, beginning again*) There once was a king, called Midas—

(*Enter* MIDAS *waving regally with both hands, wearing a tall Phrygian cap*)

SERVANT 2: (*gleefully suggesting the next line*) Whose schemes never failed to surprise us!

PRINCE: (*butting in*) His follies were endless,
So Heaven defend us

HERMES: From fools of the like of King Midas.

MIDAS: Hey! Who are you calling a fool?

HERMES: Well? You have a peaceful kingdom, a beautiful wife, a devoted little son (PRINCE *gets up and bows*), enough to eat, a soft bed to sleep in. And still you want more.

(*Exit* PRINCE *and* SERVANTS)

MIDAS: That's not foolish. That's . . . *human nature.* (*Points to* SILENUS) Now *there's* a fool, if we're talking >fools! Yesterday he drank two flagons of wine and today he can't tell his hooves from his helbow – can't even find his way out of my garden . . . *And* he's one of your lot.

HERMES: A satyr, actually.

MIDAS: (*goes to rouse* SILENUS *and help him up*) Come on, Silenus. Lean on me. I'll point you in the right direction for Olympus.

(*He helps* SILENUS *around the stage, while* SILENUS *keeps up continuous, drunken expressions of thanks*)

Here you are. This path will take you home.

SILENUS: Sho kind. What a friend! Marvellush! Wanna thank . . . how can I thank you? Lemme thank you!

MIDAS: (*extricating himself*) Don't mention it.

SILENUS: Give you a wish. Do wishes, I do. Wishawish, Midash. Midash wishawish. (*Intrigued by the sound of the words*) Midashwishawish! Gwon! Jush for Shilenush! Wishawish!

MIDAS: All right, all right. I'll wish. I wish that . . . I wish that everything I touch would turn to gold.

SILENUS: Oooooooo. Shillywish. Wishagain, Midash.

(MIDAS *stands firm*)

Shillyshillywish. (*Trotting off*) You'll be shorry!

(*Chime-bar chord. After a moment,* MIDAS *performs an Alakazam-type gesture over the floor, to no effect*)

MIDAS: (*to audience*) So much for satyrs, eh? What a wish that would have been, though! Every plate in my kitchens – GOLD! Every sword in my armoury – GOLD! Every brick in my walls. Every base drachma in my pocket . . .

(*He thrusts his hands into his pockets – chime-bar chord – and pulls out gold coins*)

. . . Nah.

(*We can see him wondering, not daring to believe.
Reaches to pick up the stone – chime-bar chord – and
turns the stone in lifting it to show underside painted
gold. Gives a cry of ecstasy. Runs off. Runs back across
the stage and into other wings, brandishing gold cutlery
at the audience. Runs back across brandishing a gold
plate. Dances back, giggling, with fistfuls of golden
chocolate coins which he throws into the audience. Off
again. Comes back wearing 'heavy' gold version of
Phrygian cap, walking bow-legged, but still happy*)

Bring me breakfast! Being rich makes me hungry!

(*Enter* SERVANT I, *who mimes bringing a plate of food.*
MIDAS *picks up a supposed chicken leg and bites into it
– chime-bar chord*)

Ow! Ow! I broke a tooth! Ow! A drink, someone! I've cut
my mouth!

(*Exit* SERVANT I. *Enter* SERVANT 2 *with mime cup.*
MIDAS *mimes drinking – chime-bar chord – he shakes
the cup upside down. Starts to look frightened.* SER-
VANT I *brings on a bunch of grapes half-gilded (non-
gilded side to the audience), and, while speaking, holds
them high for* MIDAS *to nibble from*)

SERVANT I: Suddenly Midas was ravenous, and as thirsty
as sand. He tried every way to outwit his wish,

(*Chime-bar chord.* SERVANT I *twirls grapes round so
that gold side shows*)

but it stuck to his skin like tar. From head to foot, he had
been tarred and feathered in magic.

SERVANT 2: When he walked through his gardens now, the
flowerheads banged about his knees (*cowbell bongs*), their
stiff stems prodded him. Their perfume was the same as the
bricks in his palace wall. His clothes clanged round him like
a bell round its clapper.

MIDAS: (*grabbing hold of* SERVANT 2 – *chime-bar chord – who freezes, like a statue*) Well, do something, can't you? . . . O Zeus! What have I done?

SERVANT 1: Midas threw himself down on his bed.

(MIDAS *does so (no bed needed) – cymbal clash*)

Like a golden sarcophagus, the bedclothes clamped him. He would have wept into his pillow, but his pillow spurned him, rock hard.

(MIDAS *tries to 'plump' his pillow but hurts himself doing it*)

He tried to wash the gift from his hands.

(MIDAS *mimes washing – chime-bar chord*)

but the water in the bowl bruised his fingertips. More solid than ice.

PRINCE: (*running on, arms outstretched*) Daddy! Daddy! Daddy! Have you seen the horses?

MIDAS: No! No, no, son! Stay away!

PRINCE: The stable doors are all golden, and inside, the horses—

MIDAS: Don't touch me, son! Don't!

(*The* PRINCE *clasps hold of his father's hand – chime-bar chord – and freezes into a statue*)

NO!

QUEEN: (*entering*) Midas locked himself in his room. I could hear his tears tinkling to the floor – little golden beads of misery.

(*Tinkling chime-bar downward glissando*)

MIDAS: How long does it take a man to starve? Or to be pressed to death by good fortune? (*Calls through cupped hands*) O ZEUS! SILENUS! I TAKE IT BACK! FORGIVE ME! I DON'T WANT IT! TAKE BACK YOUR GIFT!

SILENUS: (*sauntering on from the opposite side to the one* MIDAS *is facing*) So. You wish your wish unwished, do you, Midas?

MIDAS: (*on his knees*) Yes! Oh yes!

HERMES: (*entering*) He called you a fool, Silenus. This man with the golden touch. This man in his metal palace with a garden full of metal flowers. *He* called *you* a fool.

MIDAS: I'm sorry! I'm the world's biggest fool, I know it. But I've learned! I'll never be so stupid again, if you'll just—

(*Three different chime-bar chords*)

SILENUS: Then go and wash yourself in the river. Your

golden servants, too. Your golden horses. (*Indicates the* PRINCE) The golden apple of your golden eye.

> (MIDAS *wrestles his son rigid off stage.* SILENUS *calls after him*)

And don't forget to wash behind your ears!

> (HERMES *and* SILENUS *sit down on the front of the stage*)

A proper fool, that one.

HERMES: An eighteen-carat fool.

SILENUS: A hall-marked, mint-condition, gilt-edged, copper-bottomed fool.

HERMES/SILENUS: The crowned king of fools.

> (MIDAS *returns wearing ordinary cap (but with donkey ears hidden underneath it). He empties a bucket of paper pieces over* SERVANT 2 *who comes back to life. Exit* SERVANT 2. MIDAS *sits down exhausted, beside the* QUEEN)

QUEEN: Promise me you'll never make such a silly wish again.

> (*They embrace*)

MIDAS: Why would I? . . . But it mustn't ever get out – understand? I shall wash every brick – every flower – every spoon with the river water. There must be nothing left to show . . . nothing to fuel rumours. No one must know how close the King of Phrygia came to making a fool of himself. (*Examines hands*) Not a sign. I'm lucky.

QUEEN: (*leaving the stage*) You certainly are.

MIDAS: I can pay the servants to keep quiet. With a little luck, I can stifle any rumours before they even get started. No one need ever know.

(He yawns, takes off cap and reveals the donkey ears underneath)

After all, it wouldn't do for a king to be taken for an ass, would it?

(Exit)

Midas and the Dreaded Secret

King Midas has something to hide, but he
reckons he's got the situation covered.

Cast

KING MIDAS
his QUEEN
BATTUS THE BARBER
THE REEDS (as many as you like)

Costumes

- Midas and Queen as before
- Battus could have an apron
- Reeds could wear green

Props

- towel
- large pair of scissors
- hand mirror
- blue watery cloth
- chair

Idea!

This is an exhibition piece for two of your best actors. Lengthy speeches by King Midas and Battus might be used as test pieces for drama exams.

Wish-a-Wish and this play could, of course, be combined into a single play.

MIDAS AND THE DREADED SECRET

There is an ordinary chair, in the centre of an empty stage.
MIDAS *and his* QUEEN *hurry on stage, the* QUEEN *trying to smooth* MIDAS's *ruffled temper.* MIDAS *is wearing the Phrygian cap with ears under, as in 'Wish-a-Wish'.*

QUEEN: I never said I didn't like it, dear. It's a very nice cap. A lovely cap.

MIDAS: What then? What's the matter with wearing a cap?

QUEEN: Nothing! Not a thing, dear. Do calm down, dear. I only asked why you were wearing it in bed. I mean, doesn't your head need a rest – a breather? Shouldn't you let the air get to your . . .

MIDAS: I don't breathe through the top of my head, do I?

QUEEN: No, dear. Forget I mentioned it. I never meant to upset you.

MIDAS: That's all right, then. Let us hear no more about it. If I choose to wear a cap—

QUEEN: And it is a very nice cap, dear . . .

MIDAS: —it is nobody's business but my own. I think you'll agree?

QUEEN: Of course, dear . . . And I'm sure the barber will manage somehow.

MIDAS: The barber? Did you say the barber?

QUEEN: Yes, dear. Battus the Barber. He's outside waiting. I'll send him in.

(*Exit* QUEEN)

MIDAS: No! Tell him I don't want . . . Ohwaah. Battus? He's the worst gossip in Phrygia! What am I going to do now? I could send him away . . . but then he might smell a rat. I've kept it from everyone up until now. The cap hides . . . everything. But the barber? Doh! Should I say I've taken a vow never to cut my hair? I've heard of people doing that. Oh Zeus! I know I was a fool over the business of the gold . . . but did I really deserve *this*? A king needs dignity! A king needs to command respect! A king needs to be taken *seriously*!

(*Puts hands to cap as if to take it off. Enter* BATTUS THE BARBER, *briefly*)

Go away! I'm not ready!

(*Exit* BATTUS *at a run*)

I know! I'll issue a decree that everyone in Phrygia – every grown male – has to wear a cap like mine. Yes! I'll make it the national costume! Soon no one will feel fully dressed unless they are wearing one. I shall set the Minister of Propaganda to work on it.

'If you want to get ahead, get a hat!'

'Don't leave home without a coxcomb!'

'Only a sap goes out without a cap!'

'You'd be insane / To bare your mane / To wind and rain!'

Yes, yes, yes! Everyone will be wearing hats! No one will even bother to wonder why I never take off mine . . .

(*Enter* BATTUS *cautiously, holding large scissors, hand mirror and towel*)

BATTUS: Is one ready for me yet, Majesty?

MIDAS: (*aside*) This chatterer. This gossip-monger. He takes scandal round from house to house, like a milkman delivering milk. Everyone confides their secrets to a barber . . . then the barber confides them to everyone else! (*To* BATTUS) No! Go away! I'm too busy. Come back tomorrow – in a week – next month.

BATTUS: But, Majesty. One's hair is gravely in need. One's hair is becoming unruly – dishevelled, even. Dare one say it – a sight.

(*Offers the mirror for* MIDAS *to look*)

MIDAS: Yes, yes. Be that as it may. I'm too busy this morning. Go away.

BATTUS: (*aside*) This is bad. Has he found himself a new barber, I wonder? Oooo, I'd never live it down. I'd be ruined.

MIDAS: After all, it's my hair, isn't it? I suppose I may do as I like with it?

BATTUS: Oh *absolutely*, Majesty. But shan't I just comb one through? After all, one has nits to consider . . . urticaria, itchis scalpia, alopecia . . . fleabitus . . . (*Aside, as* MIDAS *starts to scratch*) Works every time. (*To* MIDAS) A scalp massage, Majesty! Shall I just give one a nice scalp massage? Very soothing. Very stimulating to the brain. That cap, after all . . . it must constrict the blood supply . . .

MIDAS: All right! All right! You may cut my hair!

BATTUS: Oh, I do think one is very wise. I was saying to Lady Euthanasia only the other day . . .

MIDAS: But first I want a promise from you.

BATTUS: A promise, Majesty?

MIDAS: Of absolute discretion.

BATTUS: Who? Me? One should know by now, I am the very soul of discretion. How can one doubt it? (*Aside to audience*) Ah! Now I've sussed him! He's found a bald spot! The King is losing his hair! That's what this cap business is all about! Midas is getting thin on top!

MIDAS: And no laughing.

BATTUS: (*po-faced*) Laugh, sire? I'll have one know, I didn't laugh even when Lady Denticaria took to wearing stuffed birds on her head and got jumped on by her own cat. We barbers take a professional pride in being discreet. Nothing you could show me would even startle me, let alone make me laugh.

MIDAS: . . . or talk! Because if this gets out . . .

BATTUS: Sire! Nothing one says will go beyond these four walls. On my mirror and scissors I swear it! (*Aside*) The vanity of these royals! You'd think no one had ever lost his hair before.

MIDAS: (*sitting down on chair*) And remember . . . no laughing, right?

BATTUS: No laughing.

(MIDAS *takes off hat, revealing ass's ears.* BATTUS *goes through great contortions of face and body, trying not to laugh, finally shoves towel in his mouth and leaves it there*)

MIDAS: It was a wicked practical joke practised on me by the gods. I didn't deserve it.

(BATTUS *shakes his head vigorously*)

Sometimes the gods can be very cruel.

(BATTUS *nods just as vigorously*)

Well? Get on with it. Cut my hair. Close and short. I don't want to be taking off my cap any more than I have to.

(BATTUS *hangs towel round* MIDAS*'s neck and starts to snip at his hair as they move off stage.*

Re-enter BATTUS *after a moment, alone, flapping towel, still holding mirror*)

BATTUS: Oh! Ow! Ouch! I think I've wrenched something, laughing. Zeus! I thought I'd die. I may still. Oh wait till I tell Xanthus! Wait till he hears . . . oh, but I can't! My oath. I swore. And if it gets out – you-know-what – Midas will know I let his secret out of the bag . . . Oh, I don't know what to do! I'll ask my wife. She'll know . . . Oh, but then I'd be telling her, too! . . . Still, that couldn't hurt, could it? Ethra can keep a secret . . . (*Looks into mirror, conducts a conversation with his reflection*) Are you out of your mind?

Well, what would *you* do?

What would I do? I'd tell someone, that's what!

Pull yourself together, Battus. Put it out of your mind.

Just because the King has got two dirty great . . . (*Looks around, scared*) Oops. Must watch my tongue. You never know who might be listening. Put it out of mind, yes. Easy, really. Just don't mention ears. Keep off the subject of ears . . . NEXT!

(*A member of the audience is 'escorted' to the barber's chair.* BATTUS *puts a towel round him and mimes cutting*)

Good to see you again, sir. How's tricks? (*Aside*) I can do this. I can do this. (*To customer*) What is it today, then, sir? Shall I leave it long over the ears? Aagh! Nice outfit, sir. Very modish. You can't beat a well-cut donkey jacket . . . Urcgh! Hasn't this rain been just terrible? I was saying to the King this morning: nice weather for donkeys . . . Eeek! Take no notice, sir. Just my little way. Business good? No? Tell me about it! I blame the politicians, eh? Most of the time they're just talking out of their asses . . . (*Laughs hysterically, ending with an ee-haw noise*) I'm sorry! You'll have to forgive me, sir. Come back tomorrow. I'm sorry. I'm sorry.

(*Gags himself with the towel and runs off stage, while 'customer' returns to the audience.*

Passage of time. Re-enter BATTUS, *banging his forehead with one palm*)

It's hopeless. I'm exhausted. I daren't even sleep at night, in case I talk in my sleep and say that King Midas has long . . . (*Groans*) I've just got to tell someone – somebody – some*thing*. (*Tries telling the mirror*) King Midas has long . . . No, it's no good. You already know.

(*Picks up chair and goes off again. Enter the* REEDS, *carrying a strip of blue watery cloth. They range themselves across the back of the stage, wafting the*

cloth. All REEDS *curl up except for the one at either end*
– REEDS 1 *and* 2. *Re-enter* BATTUS *empty-handed*)

REED 1: At last Battus the Barber went down to the river.

REED 2: The river where, once, foolish King Midas had washed off his terrible gift of golden magic.

BATTUS: Ooo, I'm in torment! I can't bear it! Should I tell my secret to the river? No! It might travel all the way down to the sea and crash about in the surf. But it's burning holes in me! I must be rid of it! Perhaps I should throw *myself* in the river. That would keep me quiet.

(*Gears himself up to take a running jump, but stops short. Groans. Then, inspiration!*)

I know! I'll dig a hole, here in the river bank. A deep, deep hole.

(BATTUS *digs with his hands, back to audience*)

REED 1: Down he digs, deep and deeper, into the dark earth.

REED 2: Then, pushing his head underground, he whispers the words that have so wanted to be spoken, the secret he has so longed to share.

(REEDS 1 *and* 2 *also curl up*)

BATTUS: (*stage whisper*) King Midas has long ass's ears!

(*Sits down, hugely relieved*)

There now. It's said. I've got it out of me. Phew! What a relief. It's gone. Forgotten. My! What a weight off my shoulders! (*Pats the ground*) My secret, safe underground. Now perhaps I can get back to work.

(*Exit* BATTUS *at one side of stage. At the same moment,*
MIDAS *enters from the other*)

MIDAS: Now perhaps I can get back to work. Phew! What

a relief. (*Explains to audience*) Everyone is wearing them. Quite the fashion craze! No one feels properly dressed unless he's wearing a tall Phrygian cap just like the King's. I'm brilliant. I'm a genius. My reputation is safe . . . And amazingly, Battus the Barber has been true to his word: not a breath of a rumour anywhere. What an excellent man! Excellent.

(*He withdraws to the side of the stage, where the* QUEEN *enters and chats to him.* BATTUS *eases back onto far side of stage*)

REED 1: And down by the river, the secret lies buried in the bank – all winter and most of the spring.

REED 2: Along with other, older secrets.

REED 1: For every moist river bank holds secrets by the million, if you think about it.

ALL REEDS: Seeds! The seeds of the reeds.

(*The* REEDS *'grow' little by little, first raising one finger, then one arm, then standing up, then reaching upwards, swaying in unison. Their speech is sibilant*)

See the rushes pricking through,
Groping for the sky's spring blue.
Growing imperceptibly:
Tall as an ankle, tall as a knee;
Tall as a waist and tall as heads:
Serried grow the osier beds.
See them sway, as up they grow;
See them toss as soft winds blow;
See them sway, as up they grow;
See them toss as soft winds blow;
Hear them whisper what they know:
KING MIDAS HAS LONG ASS'S EARS!
KING MIDAS HAS LONG ASS'S EARS!
KING MIDAS HAS LONG ASS'S EARS!

(QUEEN, *in disbelief, pulls off* MIDAS*'s cap. The* REEDS
all point at MIDAS)

KING MIDAS HAS LONG ASS'S EARS!

(*Everyone scatters off stage, all but* MIDAS *laughing*)

Iason and the Jargonauts

An epic journey in search of the Golden Fleece . . . and someone who can spell.

Cast

SECOND-IN-COMMAND

JASON

ARGONAUTS A to E (strictly speaking these should include HERAKLES and THESEUS, as elsewhere); more if desired

MEDEA

Costumes

- cloak covered in cabalistic signs for Medea

Props

- throne
- sword
- golden fleece
- small bottle
- toy lamb

Special Effects

- crash of breaking glass
- silent-movie chase music (optional)

Idea!

Explore further the adventures of the Argonauts and decide which of them would make an effective play.

IASON AND THE JARGONAUTS

The throne stands to one side of the stage with the Golden Fleece draped over it like a seat-cover. SECOND-IN-COMMAND *takes up his position centre stage, at the front. He is going to declaim a doggerel epic. Just after he begins,* JASON *hurries across the rear of the stage, and stops to listen. The rest of the* CREW *saunter on behind him.*

SECOND: Pay heed and let me tell you of a hero strong and bold,
Who sailed across the ocean wide to steal a fleece of gold!
His name was Iason; his ship, the *Argo*, sleek and black
Sped through foam-flecked fathoms, to fetch the treasure back.
The crew Iason mustered from every far-flung shore
Were heroes of the kind the world has never seen before!

JASON: (*approaching to interrupt*) Er . . .

SECOND: There were, among their number, Herakles and Theseus,
But bravest of them all was Iason of—

JASON: Second, Second. Iason?

SECOND: Iason, yes. Prince of Thessaly.

JASON: Yes, yes, I know who I am. But what happened to 'Jason'?

SECOND: Oh, but there isn't a J in the Greek alphabet. So it must have been Iason really. Excuse me.
But bravest of them all was Iason of—

JASON: Yes, but we've been translated, haven't we.

SECOND: We have?

JASON: Yes. Anyway – everyone knows it's Jason and the Golden Fleece. (*To audience*) Don't you?

SECOND: So it's J for I, right?

JASON: Right. Carry on. Haven't got all day.

SECOND: Iason, son of . . . sorry. Jason, son of Jeson was the rightful prince of—

JASON: What? Who's Jeson? My father's name was Aeson. King Aeson.

SECOND: Yes, but . . . I thought . . .

JASON: Jason, son of Aeson. It's not an I, it's an AE.

SECOND: Ah! Very good, captain. Jason, son of Aeson, King of Jolcus.

JASON: Iolcus! Ohwww . . . let's just show them, shall we?

SECOND: I thought you were in a hurry.

JASON: Well, we'll just have to show them quickly. Right.

(*He grabs members of the* CREW *and makes them characters in his fast-moving story. Grabs* A *and plonks him into the throne*)

My father is rightful King of Iolcus. But he is supplanted by his wicked brother . . . Pelias

(*Hoiks* A *out of throne and plonks* B *there instead*)

While I am away doing heroic things, Uncle Pelias kills my father . . .

(B *smartly stabs* A *who falls back into arms of* C *and* D *who drag him off stage, then return*)

I come back and say: 'Usurper! Murderer! You are not worthy to be King of Iolcus!' And Pelias says:

CREWMAN B [PELIAS]: Righto. If you'll just fetch me the Golden Fleece of the famous flying sheep, I'll step down.

JASON: Of course, first we have to find it. So we go to consult Blind King Phineus, crossing the wine-dark sea in our fast black ship, the *Argo*.

(*Hoiks* B *out of throne and plonks* E *down. The rest of the* CREW *array themselves round an invisible table, knees bent to look as if they are sitting*)

CREWMAN E [PHINEUS]: (*quavering elderly voice*) You are most welcome, Iason!

JASON: Now don't *you* start.

CREWMAN E: Welcome to my ragged kingdom. I shall summon a feast for you, but I fear you will go to bed hungry, for all that.

JASON: And no sooner is the table laid, than down fly the Harpies – hideous birds with the heads of women and claws like sickles – and strip the table bare . . . that's you, Second.

SECOND: (*perfunctory mime*) Oh. Sorry, captain. Flap-flap. Flap-flap. Shriek. Peck. Gobble gobble.

JASON: But the Argonauts will not be cowed by these thieving magpies! They leap up, with cries of:

CREWMAN B: 'We are Jason and the Jargonauts!'

CREWMAN C: Juggernauts.

CREWMAN D: Dreadnoughts.

CREWMAN A: (*returning on stage*) Argonauts.

JASON: Thank you. 'We are Jason and the Argonauts, and you Harpies have tormented this poor old man for the last time!'

(They chase SECOND *around the stage to the accompaniment of silent-movie chase music. They beat him up. He lies flattened at the back of the stage)*

CREWMAN [PHINEUS]: Oh, Jason! How can I ever thank you! You have rid my courts of the hideous Harpies. *(Getting carried away)* To find Colchis and the Golden Fleece just take the second star on the right and keep straight on till morning!

(All but CREWMAN E *bunch together and sway as if aboard ship)*

JASON: *(looking beset by fools)* So off we row to Colchis, crossing the wine-dark sea. And there Iason . . . you've got me doing it now. And there Jason asks for the priceless Golden Fleece from the foul tyrant, King Aeetes . . . *(to* SECOND) Not a word – not a *single word*, right?

(He ousts E *and plonks* D *into throne. Slightly more of a play begins to emerge)*

CREWMAN D [AEETES]: *(sardonic)* Oho yes, Prince Jason! Of course I shall give you my dearest possession – the greatest prize in my entire kingdom! Help yourself, do! It's hanging over a branch of that tree yonder. Take no notice of the *lidless dragon which guards it and which never sleeps.*

JASON: Thanks!

CREWMAN D: But first you must do me one small service. Harness my pair of fire-breathing oxen and sow that field with *THESE*.

(He mimes handing JASON *something – 'a bag'). (He exits laughing.*

JASON: *(mimes looking inside)* Teeth?

CREWMAN D: *(baring his teeth)* Teeth!

All the CREW *except for* SECOND *and* D *bunch together to represent the bull and charge at* JASON *who fights it like a toreador. In the last pass, he sidesteps, and it lumbers off stage with a huge noise of breaking glass.* SECOND *rises groaning to his hands and knees.* JASON *summons him and, using him 'wheelbarrow-style', ploughs the stage)*

JASON: I harness the oxen and plough the field. Then I sow the teeth, as I have been told to. (*Doing so*)

SECOND: But wherever a tooth falls, it grows and ripens in a single second, into a warrior, armed to the . . . well . . . TEETH.

(*One at a time, the* CREW *somersault on stage and spring up, roaring and brandishing invisible swords, spears, etc. A slow-motion, comic-book fight takes place, with members of the* CREW *exclaiming: 'Zap!' 'Pow!' 'Splat!' 'Biff!' 'Aaargh!', as* JASON *flattens them.*

Enter MEDEA *with a swirl of her cloak. She uses exaggerated magician's-assistant-style movements whenever she speaks)*

MEDEA: Princess Medea, daughter of the tyrannical King Jeetes, watches Iason with a beating heart.

JASON: Oh for heaven's sake! Not you, too?

MEDEA: Secretly she hates her father and wishes the Astronauts well!

CREW AND JASON: *ARGONAUTS!*

MEDEA: Quickly, Jason! Throw dust in their eyes!

(JASON *does so, and the* CREW *turn on each other, stagily blaming each other and starting to brawl. The brawl becomes more and more convincing)*

JASON: Men. Men! That's enough.

(Instead of getting up, the CREW *rise onto hands and feet and join themselves together into a sort of centipede-cum-dragon around the throne)*

MEDEA: Medea has studied the black arts, and uses her magical powers to close the dragon's lidless eyes in bottomless sleep.

*(*MEDEA *does more cloak-swirling. 'Dragon' keels over and slumps down, snoring)*

JASON: Oh, Medea!

MEDEA: Oh, Jason!

JASON: Medea!

MEDEA: Jason!

JASON: Marry me!

MEDEA: I thought you'd never ask!

(They move romantically towards each other. SECOND *struggles to his feet in between them, just as they meet. He takes fleece from over the back of the throne)*

SECOND: And so the Golden Fleece is won! We hurry aboard the *Argo* and speed once more across the wine-dark sea!

CREWMAN A: Sort of Argonoughts-and-crossings, this, isn't it?

(They bunch together and sway as if aboard ship)

SECOND: Princess Medea stands in the prow, urging the rowers on. King Aeetes gives chase, but the *Argo* outruns him.

JASON: (Don't tell them the bit about Apsyrtus. This is a family show.)

SECOND: Righto, skipper. Which brings us here, back home in Iolcus. And now Pelias will have to give up his stolen throne.

CREWMAN B: *(aside)* And there goes a flying pig.

(He resumes the role of PELIAS *and sits in throne)*

So, Jason! You have come back alive – and brought yourself home a wife, as well – how charming. But where, pray, is my Golden Fleece?

(JASON and MEDEA *produce the Golden Fleece)*

(aside) Dammit! I can see I shall have to send for my trusty assassins.

MEDEA: *(offering a bottle)* You look unwell, Lord Pelias. As your guest, may I offer you a token of my healing arts?

CREWMAN B [PELIAS]: Haha! Not so fast, young lady! I suppose you think you can poison me and take my crown that way?

(MEDEA *claps her hands. One* CREW MEMBER *(very
close to the wings) goes down on all fours; the Fleece is
draped over him)*

Observe this ewe!

CREWMAN [SHEEP]: Who, me?

MEDEA: Yes, ewe . . . Sleep, sheep!

(*She gives it a bottle to drink from. The* SHEEP *drops
down and snores. She holds her cloak in front of it. Exit*
SHEEP/CREWMAN. *Sheep is replaced with a toy lamb.*
MEDEA *removes the cloak)*

Behold! Mutton dressed as lamb!

CREWMAN B [PELIAS]: (*to audience*) The elixir of youth!
The woman can make the old young again! (*To* MEDEA)
Give me some! Let me drink! You said I could!

MEDEA: By all means, Uncle. Drink deep.

(PELIAS *snatches the bottle and drinks. Yawns and
staggers. Heads back towards his throne but does not
quite make it before subsiding)*

CREWMAN B [PELIAS]: First I'll sleep. And then I'll wake.
Young again! What can't I do when I'm young again!

(*He sleeps, propped up against side of throne)*

JASON: Medea, what have you done?

MEDEA: I have sent your uncle to sleep – as I did the sheep.

JASON: And when he wakes up again, will he . . . ?

MEDEA: Did I say anything about him waking up again?

(*This takes a while to sink in, then the* CREW *look
pleased and lug* PELIAS *off stage)*

JASON: (*rubbing his hands*) So! The kingdom's mine!

MEDEA: This? Huh! Give it to Pelias's son. I can find you a better kingdom than this. You shall have Corinth! With my help, you shall have anything our hearts desire. Nothing and nobody will stand in our way.

(*Exit* MEDEA. JASON *watches her go, thoughtful*)

JASON: Mmmm. Hard lady.

CREWMAN C: There was that business with Apsyrtus.

REST OF CREW: Shshshsh! This is a family show.

SECOND: But you wouldn't change her for all the world, would you, captain? Not a *priestess of Hecate*? With a good line in *black magic*?

(JASON *ignores him, lost in thought. Exit* JASON.
SECOND *shrugs*)

Oh, well. Come on, Astronauts: all aboard the *Argo*.

(*Exit* SECOND, *followed by rest of* CREW)

The Good Doctor

Asclepius keeps a snake in his pocket and healing
in his hands. In fact he is such a good doctor that,
if he set his mind to it, he could almost wake the
dead . . .

Cast

SICKNESS

ZEUS

EAGLE OPERATORS

APOLLO

ASCLEPIUS

several CROWD MEMBERS including ATHLETE, WORRIER, SOLDIER, CHILDLESS WOMAN, MOTHER and DAUGHTER, GIRL

ARTEMIS

ORION (non-speaking PLUTO)

someone at back of audience

someone in wings to catch wand

Costumes
• gods as elsewhere
• crescent moons in Artemis's hair or on her clothes
• mask for Sickness (same as in *Pandora's Box*, if plays are performed together)

Props
• eagle gloves
• Prometheus dummy, as in *Stolen Fire* (if plays are performed together)
• large sock-puppet snake, in form of long glove
• bunch of herbs
• Asclepian wand
• bow painted silver, but no arrow
• thunderbolt

Special Effects

- circus music
- recording of bowstring twang

Idea!

Which other mythological Greek characters appear as constellations in the night sky?

THE GOOD DOCTOR

The tormentors of Prometheus are found stabbing away at the miniature chained dummy with their eagle gloves (see 'Stolen Fire'). [Alternatively they are already standing one to each side of the stage; adjust the opening speech if this play is to stand alone.]

(*Enter* SICKNESS *dressed as in 'Pandora's Box'*)

SICKNESS: (*jerking a thumb at Prometheus but talking to the audience, menacing*) How's he feeling? Not too good . . .
So things are going as they should.
How're *you* feeling? Feeling fine?
Have some remedies of *mine.*
Think that we've already met?
Babe, you ain't seen nothing yet.
I am Sickness. Here's to me!
Master of the malady.
Since I skipped Pandora's Box
I have doled out chicken pox,
Mumps and gout and fits and flu,
Plague and fevers – migraines, too . . .
Now I'm coming after YOU! (*Makes to climb off front of stage*)
What d'you mean, 'I make you sick?'
That, sir, is my party trick.

(*Exit* SICKNESS *stage left, sniggering. Enter* ZEUS. *He whistles to the* EAGLES *and deploys them to either side of the stage*)

ZEUS: Early in the history of the world, my son Apollo

asked where exactly its centre was. So I released twin eagles from either end of the world. Where they met was . . .

(*The* EAGLES *meet mid-stage. Enter* APOLLO, *leaping onto the same spot with a hop, skip and jump. On his arm he is wearing a long green glove in the form of a snake*)

APOLLO: DELPHI! The Centre of the World!

ZEUS: And since my son Apollo always thinks of himself as Centre of the Universe, he of course made Delphi his own.

APOLLO: I sited there the Delphic Oracle—

(*He shows snake like a ventriloquist showing his dummy. Circus music. Enter large* CROWD *of people from all sides. They react identically to each of the Oracle's pronouncements*)

And the Delphic Oracle spoke. 'Hello, evvygoggy. Gockle of geer.' People came from all over the world, bringing their problems with them. The Delphic Oracle, you see, spoke strange words— (*Listens to snake then translates in a snakey voice*) Discombobulate.

CROWD: Ooooo!

APOLLO: Gingko biloba!

CROWD: Wheee!

APOLLO: Amphigoric blatherskite!

CROWD: Ahhhh!

(APOLLO *listens, then slaps the snake's nose as if it has said something outrageous.* SICKNESS *passes among the* CROWD *sprinkling disease. People begin to cough, sneeze, hold their heads, etc. Then he goes and sits on the front of the stage, unobtrusive*)

APOLLO: . . . though her language was often difficult to understand . . . (*Listens and translates*) *It's a googly and he's edged a full toss down to silly mid-off to break his duck!*

CROWD: Uh?

APOLLO: Still, everyone received an answer of some sort.

ATHLETE: Shall I win a laurel wreath at the Pythian Games?

APOLLO: (*snakey voice*) The one who runs fastest and jumps highest will win the laurel.

> (ATHLETE *looks enlightened, then baffled. Exit* ATHLETE)

WORRIER: When will I die?

APOLLO: (*snakey voice*) At the end of your life.

WORRIER: No, I meant shall I live to a great age?

APOLLO: (*snakey voice*) The stars will live longer.

> (*Reaction as before. Exit* WORRIER)

SOLDIER: Will Athens win against the Boeotians in tomorrow's battle?

> (APOLLO *flops snake's head downwards and lets it hang there limply. Exit* SOLDIER)

CHILDLESS WOMAN: Will I ever have a son?

APOLLO: (*snakey voice*) Apollo and Coronis will! (*In his own voice, grabbing snake with other hand*) *Apollo will? What d'you mean, 'Apollo will'?*

ZEUS: But of course the Oracle always spoke the truth. Soon Asclepius was born – a boy with a name as difficult as a doctor's handwriting but a nature as sweet as balm.

> (*Enter* ASCLEPIUS *with bunch of herbs. During the next speeches he moves among the coughing, feverish*

CROWD *distributing herbs and concern. The people
look happier and gradually leave*)

He was the apple of his father's eye.

APOLLO: (*fondly*) The apple of my eye. Foolish boy. He
carries snakes around in his pockets, you know, to help him
hunt out healing herbs? Spends whole days grinding and
mixing potions and lotions . . .

MOTHER: (*to Oracle, clutching* DAUGHTER) Will my
daughter ever be rid of this cough?

APOLLO: (*snakey voice*) She won't cough after she is dead.

(MOTHER *and* DAUGHTER *make to leave, upset.*
ASCLEPIUS *intercepts them*)

ASCLEPIUS: Perhaps if you make an infusion of balsam and
have her breathe it in? And a little camphorated oil rubbed
on to her chest at night?

MOTHER: You are wonderful, Asclepius. So kind! So dear!
Thank you! Oh thank you!

(*Exit* MOTHER, DAUGHTER *and rest of* CROWD)

APOLLO: I don't know why you waste your time on them.
It's no great loss if a few mortals die.

ASCLEPIUS: You forget. I'm mortal, too – well, half of me
is. And I hate to see anyone suffer when there are so many
remedies just reaching out to them in the leaves and the
flowers.

APOLLO: (*fondly*) Too tender-hearted for your own good,
that's you, son.

(*A* GIRL *runs on and in dumbshow asks* ASCLEPIUS *for
help, pointing off stage*)

SICKNESS: (*facing front*) Yes, you tell him. That boy
Asclepius is doubling my work. I no sooner infect someone

with a nice disease than *he* comes along with some herb or lotion and makes them well again. He heals wounds! He dulls pain. Medicine, blah! The world did very well without medicine. Why did this *apothecary* have to interfere? Not natural!

ASCLEPIUS: (*giving something to* GIRL) It's perfectly natural. It comes from the bark of the willow. And it will take away your mother's pain.

(*Exit* GIRL, *delighted*)

SICKNESS: Owah! That boy will be the death of me!

ZEUS: Different as chalk and cheese . . . and yet Apollo doted on that boy. He gave him a present.

APOLLO: I've made you a present, Asclepius. (*Fetches wand from wings*) Whatever skills you have, this wand will magnify with magic. You see the snakes? Symbol of regeneration. And the double helix?

ASCLEPIUS: The shape of life itself. Thank you, Father! It will double the good I can do! Thank you!

ZEUS: For the first time, my son Apollo discovered that he was not the Centre of the Universe, after all. His boy Asclepius was that.

(*Enter* ARTEMIS *dancing exultantly*)

ARTEMIS: No, no! Orion is that! My love! Orion the Hunter! He's the centre of my universe!

ZEUS: My daughter.

APOLLO: (*with disgust*) My sister.

ZEUS AND APOLLO: Artemis, Goddess of the Hunt.

(*Exit* ZEUS)

APOLLO: I thought you swore never to love a 'mere man'.

ARTEMIS: I did, I did. Oh, but Orion has changed all that! I love him! He's the sun in my sky! He's the beat in my heart! He's . . . he's . . . (*She gestures to convey the wonder of Orion*)

APOLLO: There's certainly a lot of him. (*Indicates huge width*)

ARTEMIS: He's a miracle. What do you expect? Miracles *are* big.

(*She busies herself stringing her bow, so she does not hear what* APOLLO *says next to the audience*)

APOLLO: Great galumphing ox of a man. I've watched him swimming in the sea every evening. If he does breast stroke, he swamps Corinth. Look. Look at him. He's out there now. Miles out. Basking like a big blue whale.

ARTEMIS: (*coming and looking over his shoulder*) Who are you talking to? You're just jealous, you. Because Orion can shoot straighter than you.

APOLLO: Ha!

ARTEMIS: Come to think of it, *anyone* can shoot straighter than you.

APOLLO: Ha!

ARTEMIS: You're such a braggart, Apollo. You're so vain! You think you're the best lute player, the best lover, the best athlete, best archer . . .

APOLLO: (*hatching a callous plan*) I'll bet I can out-shoot you, 'O Mighty Huntress of the Moon'.

ARTEMIS: Of course you can't. Don't be ridiculous. I'm Goddess of the Hunt! Only Orion can shoot further . . . and even then, I'm more accurate.

APOLLO: Prove it. I bet you can't hit that . . . that piece of wood out there. See it?

ARTEMIS: (*peering out into auditorium*) I think I do . . .
(*Blustering*) Well of course I do.

APOLLO: That dark blob in among the waves.

ARTEMIS: I see it, I see it.

> (*The snake on* APOLLO's *arm tries to intervene.*
> APOLLO *grabs its beak*)

What did the Oracle say, brother?

APOLLO: It said . . . It said . . . 'Artemis will hit the
target.'

ARTEMIS: I didn't need your pet reptile to tell me that. You
go first.

> (APOLLO *borrows her bow, takes aim. Bow-twang
> sound-effect.* ARTEMIS *laughs in scorn*)

There you are! Miles wide! Here, let me.

> (*She takes aim and fires. Bow-twang sound-effect. Cry
> from back of auditorium*)

What was that? What have I done? Apollo? I'm cold. My
heart's turned cold like ice. What have I done, Apollo?
What have you made me do?

> (*Exit* APOLLO, *laughing.* ARTEMIS *rushes off other side
> shouting*)

NO!!

SICKNESS: (*gloatingly*) The moon had a pasty pallor to-
night, when the dawn clouds sank it,
Frenzied, it tugged at the sea like a sickbed blanket.
There on the beach lies the marvellous Orion:
Face pressed to the rocks like a woman's breast to cry on.
A white ash arrow has split his heart asunder
And Artemis has lost her dear, Titanic hunter.

> (ARTEMIS *re-enters, distraught*)

ARTEMIS: *NO!* Asclepius! Asclepius, where are you? Asclepius, come quick!

(*Enter* ASCLEPIUS *stage right. She runs and pulls at him. Meanwhile,* CROWD MEMBERS *drag on a body, stage left*)

You've got to come! Come on. You've got to help me! You're my nephew! You've got to help me!

ASCLEPIUS: Of course I'll help. What's the matter, lady? What's happened?

ARTEMIS: It's Orion! He's hurt!! He's injured! You have to heal him! You have medicines, don't you? That's what you do! You make people better!

(*Enter* ZEUS *and* PLUTO *who watch from a distance.* ASCLEPIUS *kneels to examine the body*)

ASCLEPIUS: This man is dead, Aunt.

ARTEMIS: Dead, sick. It's just two sides of the same horizon! You can fetch him back, can't you? You have the skill. Everyone says so!

CROWD: (*murmur variously*) Yes, yes. / He has the skill. / You could do it.

ASCLEPIUS: Wake the dead? I don't know.

PLUTO: Wake the dead? What are they saying? Down in the Underworld, my subjects will never rest if they see some chance of getting back across the River Styx! Hear them whispering already.

WHOLE CAST: (*whispering, faces averted*) Asclepius, Asclepius, bring us back. The Doctor can raise the dead!

PLUTO: Forbid it, brother Zeus. This mustn't happen!

SICKNESS: (*facing front*) Yes! Forbid it, Zeus! Where's the *fear* to come from if Death can be cured like a dose of diarrhoea?

ARTEMIS: You can do it, nephew! Your own father did this! You have to undo Apollo's wickedness!

ASCLEPIUS: I don't know. I suppose I can try.

ZEUS: Wake the dead? Earth would soon be so crammed that the mortals would stand shoulder to shoulder like so many stems of cress.

ASCLEPIUS: (*lifting* ORION's *head, taking up his wand*) I can close up his wounds . . . start up his heart by massage . . . restore his lungs with aconite . . .

ZEUS: (*appeals to audience*) Without Death, where is the difference between You and Us?

(*Enter* APOLLO, *no longer with snake. He sees* ZEUS *draw out a thunderbolt and approach* ASCLEPIUS, *the bolt raised like a weapon*)

APOLLO: *NO!* What are you doing? Wait!

ARTEMIS: *NO!*

ZEUS: I'm sorry, my son – daughter.

>   (*He strikes down* ASCLEPIUS *and leaves alongside*
>   PLUTO)

SICKNESS: YES! Let that be an end of all *DOCTORS!*

>   (APOLLO *grabs up wand and makes as if to rush after*
>   ZEUS. *He shouts off stage*)

APOLLO: You killed my son! You devil! You despot!
Murderer!

>   (*Flings wand after* ZEUS, *into wings (someone must
>   catch it). All freeze but for* SICKNESS *who, during his
>   last speech, grows increasingly ill*)

SICKNESS: (*to audience*) He missed, of course. That wand
of his went clear over Zeus and straight on – through the
troposphere, through the stratosphere, through the ringing,
singing music of the spheres . . . Impaled itself in the night
sky. But its magic . . . (*Shudders*) Its filthy, healing magic
has been filtering down ever since.

>   (*Remaining actors remove both bodies.* SICKNESS
>   *stands up*)

Invisible flecks of magic land
Like flecks of dust on head and hand.
Now there are doctors right and left . . .
Doctors, nurses, surgeons, vets.
(*Breaks off to cough hackingly*)
That boy will be the death of me,
That unpronounceable prodigy.
Asclepius.
(*Threatening the audience*) You heard the gods. The gods
brook no defiance.
And Death must come – even to sons and giants.

Sickness and Pain are forming an alliance.
So don't *ONE* of you take up the Healing Science!

(*Exit* SICKNESS, *limping and coughing*)

Flight

Held prisoner by the wicked King of Crete, a father and son decide to flee. But how can you escape from the top of a high tower guarded night and day?

Cast

DAEDALUS

ICARUS

KING MINOS

2 GUARDS

CHORUS of 4 or so

Costumes

- braces on Daedalus and Icarus, ready to take wings (see illustration for wings)
- crown for Minos

Props

- window frame on stand, sill decorated with birds
- stool
- couch
- 2 pairs wings
- 4 or so seagulls mounted on canes
- plate (nibbles optional)
- pot of 'melted wax' and brush

Special Effects

- bellow of Minotaur
- seagulls (optional)

Idea!

How would you shoot this, if you were telling the story in a movie?

FLIGHT

*Window and couch stand off-centre of stage, the window
flat on, concealing a stool behind it. There is a plate of
nibbles on the stool. Subhuman bellowing is heard.
Then . . .*

*Looking back to thank a supposed servant who has
brought them here,* DAEDALUS *and* ICARUS *enter breath-
less. They are carrying the wings, rolled up to look like
luggage. They stow them behind the couch.* ICARUS *is a
bored, self-centred, obnoxious adolescent.*

ICARUS: (*looking round, impressed*) Style! Sty-yle! Is this
stylish or what?

DAEDALUS: (*pooped*) One hundred and fifty-eight stairs! I
counted a hundred and fifty-eight stairs. We must be a
hundred feet up!

ICARUS: Yeah! And that palace! Rooms on top of other
rooms! Cellars underneath! Better than anything back in
Athens!

DAEDALUS: I wish I were in Athens now.

ICARUS: Why? This is the business! Beds, fruit, servants outside the door waiting to fetch us anything we ask
for.

DAEDALUS: The guards, you mean. (*'Trying the door', at
edge of wings*) It's barred. They've locked us in.

ICARUS: Wow! Take a look at that view! Stop griping!
Minos is paying you enough. I like it here. It's the business.

DAEDALUS: But why me? Why not some local builder? He
must have the best right here. Look at it – acres of two-

storey buildings, statues, wall paintings. It's not as if he's short of craftsmen.

ICARUS: (*bored*) You're supposed to be the best, aren't you? That's what you're always telling me. What's the problem? Minos wants The Great Daedalus to design his cellars, and he's willing to pay. You heard him: 'Name your price. No expense spared.'

DAEDALUS: But what's it for, this cellar, this maze, this Labyrinth I am supposed to build? Why does he need it?

ICARUS: (*picking up the plate*) What do you care? So long as he pays. Oo, look! Prawns!

(*Beastly bellows, off*)

DAEDALUS: I mean, why should you want a maze of passages so complicated that no one who goes in can ever find their way out again?

ICARUS: He told you: it's none of your business. He doesn't have to tell you what he wants it for – just that he wants it.

DAEDALUS: And that noise night and day. That terrible bellowing. Like a soul in torment.

ICARUS: I expect it's a bull somewhere. Bulls are big on Crete. Didn't you see those pictures on the wall? Acrobats somersaulting over them?

DAEDALUS: Beautiful. Stunning. Athens has nothing to match them. So why me? Why import an Athenian inventor to work on a Minoan palace? It's like importing donkeys to pull your racing chariots.

ICARUS: Look, you're a genius inventor, right? Stop belly-aching. I like it here.

DAEDALUS: That's good, son. That's good. I'm glad. At

least we'll have each other for company, eh? While I work?
That's what matters.

(ICARUS *does not respond to* DAEDALUS*'s affection,
but lies down and goes to sleep. Lights dim, if possible;
passage of time. Enter* KING MINOS *and* GUARD; *the
lights come up again*)

MINOS: You have done well, Daedalus. Your reputation
was well deserved. Your Labyrinth— *my* Labyrinth is a
miracle of complexity. I notice you do not ask me what it is
for?

DAEDALUS: I was told never to enquire, your Majesty.
Though I admit . . . I am intrigued.

MINOS: Well then, now that it is finished, I shall tell you.
What you have built is a sort of kennel. A zoo. It is for a
family member of mine, Daedalus. A mistake. My wife's
mistake. My wife Pasiphae gave birth to a . . . *thing*. I shall
not call it a monster. Every creature under Heaven has its
purpose – its uses. And, after all, blood is thicker than
water . . . You have built a cage to retain the Minotaur,
my . . . stepson. (*Pause*) I suppose there must be a secret to
this maze? A solution to the Labyrinth?

DAEDALUS: Oh yes, your Majesty! It's quite simple once
you've been told. It's just a matter of taking three turns to
the—

MINOS: And the secret lives in you. Like the beast in the
Labyrinth, it stalks the corridors of your brain. Yes?

DAEDALUS: Well, I suppose—

MINOS: So you'll agree: it would not do to . . . *mislay* you.

DAEDALUS: I'm sorry? I don't think I quite understand . . .

MINOS: I'm sure you and your son will be very comfortable. I gave orders that you should enjoy every creature
comfort.

DAEDALUS: Yes, but how long? How much longer must we stay? Icarus and I, we need to get home. Other projects, you know. Icarus must go back to school—

MINOS: Oh, but I'm afraid that's quite impossible. No, no. I can't let you leave Crete. You are the only one who knows the secret of the Labyrinth. Now, either I can kill you and your boy, or you can stay on as my honoured guests. For the rest of your life. I'm sure I can find many uses for your genius. Good day, Daedalus . . . Oh! One more snippet of information. Just in case you should think of trying to leave: the beast in the Labyrinth eats many things – fish, dogs, hare – but its favourite meat is *human flesh*. I would hate your boy Icarus to find himself . . . on the menu, as it were.

(*Full of panic and despair* DAEDALUS *runs to the window and sticks his head out, his back to audience*)

(*To* GUARD) See to it that their tower is guarded day and night. Daedalus stays till he dies.

(*Exit* MINOS *and* GUARD. ICARUS *stirs and sits up.* DAEDALUS *returns from window, picks up plate and sets it on the windowsill*)

DAEDALUS: (*in despair*) What have I done? What have I done?

ICARUS: I don't know what all the fuss is about. We can't leave: so what's the big deal? Food, drink, money. No need to work. We've got it made.

DAEDALUS: And live prisoners for the rest of our lives? Never! A man needs more than food and drink! Without our freedom what are we?

ICARUS: Rich?

DAEDALUS: We're hamsters running around in a wheel! We're canaries in a gilded cage. Look! Those birds out there are more alive than we are! At least they can come and go as they please.

(ICARUS *goes to help himself from plate*)

Leave that! It's there for a reason.

ICARUS: All right, all right. Keep your feathers on.

(ICARUS *goes back to sleep.* DAEDALUS *sits by the window, whistling to tempt the birds closer*)

DAEDALUS: Come on, my little friends. See? Cake! Bread! Prawns!

(*Lights dim, if possible; passage of time.*

DAEDALUS *crosses to look at* ICARUS *sleeping. Strokes his hair, then shakes him*)

Wake up! Icarus, wake up!

ICARUS: What is it? What's to get up for? Leave me alone . . .

DAEDALUS: Wake up, Icarus. We're leaving.

ICARUS: (*suddenly awake*) What d'you mean, leaving? How can we? The guards—

DAEDALUS: I've been making something.

(*He fetches out the wings from under* ICARUS's *bed*)

ICARUS: When? I never saw you.

DAEDALUS: While you were sleeping. Every night. Every night for two years.

(*He unwraps and holds out the wings*)

ICARUS: Wings?!

DAEDALUS: Each bird that came to the windowsill – I took one feather. Just one. Turn round and let me fasten them on.

(DAEDALUS *attaches one pair of wings to* ICARUS – *see illustration – using the brush and pot of 'hot wax'*)

ICARUS: Ow!

DAEDALUS: I'm sorry. The wax is hot. But when it sets, it will hold the wings tight to your shoulders. Now you fasten mine . . . and as you love me, make a proper job of it.

ICARUS: (*attaching* DAEDALUS'*s wings*) Wings? You must be mad! You want us to fly out of here? You've been cooped up in here too long. You're insane.

DAEDALUS: No, Icarus. Be brave. Trust me. We'll fly off Crete like the seagulls do – out and away over the sea. We shall fly all the way back to Athens. This tyrant Minos is feeding that beast with Greek boys and girls – with children no older than you, Icarus. How can we serve a master like that? I thought of killing myself, but then I thought: what would become of Icarus, of my beloved boy? One day, when I'd outlived my usefulness, Minos would kill us anyway. We have to try, don't you see? We have to try!

(*They move the window – with the stool behind it – forward to the front of the stage.* ICARUS *climbs out of window and on to the edge of the stage.* ICARUS *looks terrified. Spotlight only, if available*)

(*From 'inside'*) Now don't look down. Spread your wings and simply step off. The thing to remember— Icarus, are you listening?

ICARUS: Yes. Yes . . . But I might not want to go! Did you ever think about that? I might like it here!

DAEDALUS: The air will bear you up. The hot air over the land will lift you. But you must remember—

ICARUS: I know, I know. At midnight I change back into a chicken.

DAEDALUS: —don't fly too high. If you go too near the

sun, the wax on your shoulders could melt. Do you understand?

ICARUS: All right, all right. For pity's sake. Don't go on.

(DAEDALUS *too climbs 'outside'*)

Watch out! There's no room out here for both of us!

DAEDALUS: Fly, then, boy! Fly! Be the first boy in the history of the world to fly like a bird!

ICARUS: The first in the history of the world! Yes!

(*Steps off front of stage*)

DAEDALUS: (*not daring to look*) Icarus! Son! (*Looks down, then as if following an upward flight*) Yes! His wings held! They held! A few loose feathers. A swoop like a house martin coming out of the eaves! He's airborne! Brave boy! Ha ha! Up and away, casting a shadow like an eagle, cackling like a harpy. Oh, my brave boy! He's free! (*Fondly*) Look at the seagulls making way for him. See how the thermals lift him! Look at him swimming in the golden air like a trout leaping upstream!

(*Bellow off*)

The beast in the basement is restless. It can see up through the gratings – the blue sky, a boy on the wing. (*Calling*) Don't fly too high, Icarus! Remember what I said! Remember about the sun! (*Sudden fright*) They've seen him! The guards have seen him. (*Relief*) Look at them. They don't believe their eyes. A boy flying. Ha ha! What can they do? That one's so busy gaping that he walked into a tree! 'Tell the King! Tell the King!' they're shouting. Tell him his prisoners are flying away! Free of you now, Minos!

(DAEDALUS *jumps off front of stage. Enter* GUARDS, *running, one holding a bloody handkerchief to his nose*)

GUARD 1: Well, DO something!

GUARD 2: Do something yourself!

GUARD 1: Sound the alarm! Find a bow and arrow!

GUARD 2: They're out of range already. Might as well shoot at robins.

GUARD 1: Look at them.

GUARD 2: The nerve of the Greeks!

GUARD 1: Catch me.

(They stare upwards for a few moments)

Minos will have our hides for this.

GUARD 2: He will, too.

GUARD 1: There's a boat down at the harbour. If we go now, we might just get away with our skins.

GUARD 2: Beats flying.

GUARD 1: Beats dying.

GUARD 2: Let's go.

(They exit, removing the window.

Enter CHORUS *holding seagulls on the end of canes.*
They sit down as ICARUS *enters.* ICARUS *cruises round*
the stage, arms out, aeroplane-style)

ICARUS: Neeeeeowwwww! First boy in the world! First person ever to fly! Neeeeeoowwwww! There's the coast, look. Jagged, like a nibbled biscuit. And the sea smooth as metal! Miniature ships. The people – they're nothing! Ants! I could stamp them all out of existence with one foot! Out of my way, seagulls! Puny objects! Make way for Icarus, the winged boy! Ha ha! I'm one of the eagles of Zeus! I'm Hermes! What's the matter, Father? Scared of heights? What did you say? Can't hear you. You'll have to speak up! . . . Picture it when I get home. Imagine their faces when I come swooping in over the treetops. Icarus the aerial acrobat! Icarus bird-man! What you looking at, Sun? Never seen a Greek up this close before? (*Pulls a face*) Nahnanahnah! Think you're cock of the sky, don't you? Big orange face grinning down. Think you're so great, don't you? Look at you. Clippety-clop. Hack nags sent on the same ride every day. Got to be home by night-time has-oo? Mustn't stay out late. Not me! I can go on flying till midnight! Pull the stars out of the sky, that's me – throw them at the dolphins. Look at me, Father! Bet I can fly higher than you. Bet I can fly higher than the Sun, even! What? You'll have to shout. I can't hear you.

CHORUS: The seagulls drop away to either side.
Beneath the turquoise water dark shapes glide.
The air is thin and scented now, besides,
With warming wax which, like tears cried,
Begins to slip and drip around inside
His sweaty clothes. O Icarus, your pride!

Your foolish, childish, bragging, fatal pride!
The Sun will pluck your wingless, worthless hide.
The Laws of Nature will not be denied!

DAEDALUS: (*from in front of stage, calling up*)
Go down! Go down! O would that I had died!
Sooner than see you fall, my son, my pride!
My son: the sun! My son: the sun! My son!

(*The* CHORUS *rip the wings off* ICARUS *and carry them
off stage.* ICARUS *screams a long, chilling scream and
'falls' off the edge of the stage. Enter the 2 runaway*
GUARDS)

GUARD 1: We saw it from our ship, that one figure falling.

GUARD 2: That other circling in the sky.

GUARD 1: From a distance it sounded like gulls shrieking.

GUARD 2: But it wasn't.

BOTH GUARDS: It was Icarus, falling.

GUARD 2: And his father watching.

GUARD 1: The captain of our ship headed for the spot, but
there was nothing to see.

GUARD 2: Just a few feathers floating on the waves.

GUARD 1: And his father circling overhead.

(*Exit* GUARDS. *Enter* KING MINOS. *Moves to centre
front. Bellowing, off*)

MINOS: Down in the basement, the Monster is roaring. My
son. My shame. The Minotaur. Terrible shrieks, almost as if
its sharp ears heard something I couldn't. Something far out
at sea. Hush, beast, hush. Soon be feeding time. Soon. Soon.

(*Exit* MINOS, *fingers in ears*)

The Beast in the Basement

What secret horror does the King keep in his basement? And can Prince Theseus survive coming face to face with it?

Cast

KING AEGEUS, an old man

PRINCE THESEUS, his son

CHORUS – one person, or several chanting in unison, or several taking the lines in turn, as desired

several TRIBUTES bound for Crete (probably not 13, though)

KING MINOS

ARIADNE

THE MINOTAUR

2 GUARDS

Costumes

- crowns for Aegeus and Minos
- gold brow-bands for Prince Theseus and Ariadne
- bull's head for Minotaur

Props

- throne
- window
- dagger
- large reel of thread (like a kite bobbin)

Special Effects

- bellow of Minotaur
- seagulls (optional)

Idea!

The fight with the Minotaur needs to be worked out move by move.

THE BEAST IN THE BASEMENT

Window and throne are on stage. The CHORUS *(whether one person or several) stands stage front left, facing out towards audience throughout the play.* THESEUS *is looking out of the window. His father,* AEGEUS, *sits in throne.*

(*Bloodcurdling bellow offstage, followed by chilling scream. The actors do not react*)

THESEUS: Where are they going?

AEGEUS: To Crete, son. To Crete.

CHORUS: Better not to ask, Theseus. Better not to ask.

THESEUS: But why, Father? Why every year? Seven maidens and seven men. Why do we send them there? Why are the ship's sails black?

CHORUS: Better not to ask, Theseus. Better not to ask.

AEGEUS: A tribute, I told you. We offended King Minos. He demands tribute. And since he has ships enough to control the Central Sea, we must go on sending tribute. And that's what he demands. Seven maidens and seven young men, once a year.

THESEUS: But what does he want them for? Slaves? Hostages? Do they ever come back?

CHORUS: Better not to ask, Theseus. Better not to ask.

AEGEUS: I'm busy. I can't sit here explaining matters of state to you.

THESEUS: What? What aren't you telling me? Why can't I know? I'm your son, aren't I? When I'm King I'm not putting fourteen Athenians into a ship and sending them to some unknown fate! Does Minos kill them?

(*He goes to sit at his father's feet*)

CHORUS: Better not to ask, Theseus. Better not to ask.

AEGEUS: Not Minos, no. Not himself . . . He has the Minotaur to do that. There is a maze of passageways under the Minoan palace. They were designed by an Athenian – Daedalus – and he designed them with all his Greek cunning. In this Labyrinth, King Minos keeps his secret – a 'pet' – a beast – something monstrous – something white-eyed for want of sunlight . . . something *horned* . . . It has to eat.

THESEUS: No!

AEGEUS: Half man and half bull it is. Less bull than man, though. After all, bulls have no taste for human flesh.

THESEUS: (*running to the window and calling out of it*) Heave to! Don't let that ship sail! Have the captain wait. Tell him Prince Theseus is sailing with him. Set one of the tributes free. I shall take his place.

AEGEUS: Theseus, no! You don't realise! It would be suicide!

CHORUS: Rash Prince Theseus, rash as fire.
Quick as kindling: strange desire
Rushing to meet a fate so dire.
Rash Prince Theseus, rash as fire.

AEGEUS: The Minotaur will kill you!

THESEUS: Not if I kill it first! Trust me! Keep watch for me. I won't fail. If I come home victorious, I'll drop those damnable black sails and hoist white ones instead! Big white sails bellying out, full of glory!

AEGEUS: Theseus, no!

(*Exit* THESEUS. AEGEUS *goes after him, remonstrating*)

CHORUS: Cool the breeze on the open ship.
Thirteen shed salt tears.
The sea heaves: nauseous yaw and dip,
But Theseus shows no fear.

(*The scene is now Knossos, Crete. Enter* MINOS *who takes his place in the throne. Unearthly bellow, off*

Enter the TRIBUTES, *including* THESEUS)

MINOS: (*rubbing his hands gleefully*) Ah! Here you are, then. Athens's tributes. More friends for my pet to play with. More explorers for my Labyrinth. Welcome to Knossos one and all. Who will be the first to savour the delights of my basement?

CHORUS: The beast in the basement is hungry.
Two weeks since it was fed.
The palace smells of death and decay
And blood that the beast has shed.
The Labyrinth's lanes are lightless –
Complex as knotted rope.
Those who go in are sightless
Of hand or help or hope.

THESEUS: I will, Minos! I, Prince Theseus of Athens. And I shall wring the neck of this mooncalf of yours!

MINOS: Prince Theseus? Is Aegeus so short of young men that he must send his own kin, now? Or are you such a thorn in his side that he wants to be rid of you?

(THESEUS *is not listening. He has seen* ARIADNE *and is bowing, kissing her hand, engaging her in mimed conversation*)

Ariadne! No talking to the prisoners.

THESEUS: Oh, but your daughter is so much better company than you are, Minos.

MINOS: Ariadne! Don't waste your breath on them. They are without rank or future. In fact, they are so much dog meat. Guards! Take them away! . . . And search them for weapons. I would not like my Minotaur to cut his mouth in chewing on them.

(*The* GUARDS *herd* THESEUS *and* TRIBUTES *into a corner of the stage where they clutch imaginary prison bars. Bellow offstage*)

Don't you hear? My pet is hungry!

(*Exit* MINOS *and* GUARDS)

CHORUS: But Princess Ariadne
Is deaf to her father's sneer.
In low whispers the Princess bade the
Athenians not to fear.

ARIADNE: (*to* THESEUS) Wait for me by the prison window. I must speak to you.

(*Exit* ARIADNE)

CHORUS: For poor, plain Ariadne,
Not five short minutes since,
Fell truly, deeply and madly
In love with the handsome Prince.

(*All the* ATHENIANS *except* THESEUS *mop and mow with misery.* ARIADNE *creeps in and crosses to* THESEUS)

ARIADNE: If I help you tomorrow, will you take me away with you – off Crete – back to Athens?

THESEUS: (*being dashing*) I'll do better than that! I'll marry you and make you Queen of Athens one day!

ARIADNE: Oh! Oh, Theseus! You won't be sorry! Here.

Take this. (*Gives him reel of thread*) When you enter the Labyrinth, fasten the end to the door and pay it out as you go. Without it, you could roam the passageways for ever looking for the way out . . . That's if the Minotaur doesn't kill you.

THESEUS: If it finds me, I shall kill it with my bare hands!

ARIADNE: (*giving him a dagger*) This might be better . . . I must go. If my father sees me . . . I'll wait for you on the beach. Good luck, dear heart! The gods smile on you!

CHORUS: The beast in the basement is hungry.
It scents its meat on the way.
And empties its bellowing, reeking lungs
With calling for its prey!

(*The* GUARDS *fetch* THESEUS *'out of prison' and drag him stage right. Unbolting a supposed door, they throw him off stage*)

GUARD 1: Dinner is served, beast!

(*Exit* GUARDS. *Lights down, if possible.*

Re-enter THESEUS *holding the bobbin (probably better to do without actual thread) and feeling his way.*
MINOTAUR *emerges through back curtains stage centre. Eventually,* THESEUS'*s outstretched hands touch the* MINOTAUR'*s face. Meanwhile the* CHORUS *is speaking*)

CHORUS: Clatter of hooves in the darkness.
Drizzling snout in the darkness.
Sweltering hide in the darkness.
Leathery lips in the darkness.
Crescent of horn in the darkness.
Big as a plough in the darkness.
Calloused hands in the darkness –
Just like a man's in the darkness,
Heartbeats race in the darkness,
Breathing as one in the darkness,

Minotaur man can you feel it?
Death in the shape of a man.

> (*The* MINOTAUR *has* THESEUS *on the ground and is
> about to stamp on him when* THESEUS *stabs him.
> Wounded, the monster is pitiable. It whimpers.*
> THESEUS *stabs it repeatedly, then mimes the following
> lines as they are spoken*)

All alone in the darkness,
Feels for the thread in the darkness,
Wildly gropes in the darkness,
Finds only slime on the floor.
Chances on thread in the darkness,
Offers up thanks in the darkness,
Stumbles away through the darkness
And finds his way to the door.

THESEUS: And the door ajar! She must have come and shot
back the bolts. Clever girl!

(Exit stage right.

Lights up, if possible. Re-enter THESEUS, *runs to free
the* TRIBUTES)

Quick! Don't make a sound. If we can reach the harbour
before we're missed, we can be over the horizon before
Minos even wakes up.

(They make to go stage left. ARIADNE *emerges a short
way stage right)*

ARIADNE: And me?

THESEUS: *(who had forgotten her)* Oh! Yes. Naturally.
Only hurry!

(All form a boat-bow shape with hands joined, THE-
SEUS *and* ARIADNE *at the prow. The* MINOTAUR *drags
itself painfully off stage)*

CHORUS: The beast in the basement is crying:
One last great groan of despair.
The beast in the basement is dying,
Craving moonlight and salty air.

But off the Cretan coastline,
A black ship crosses the bar,
White salt caking its bowline
And sails as black as tar.

ARIADNE: Oh, Theseus, I'm so happy!

THESEUS: Free of your father's tyranny at last?

ARIADNE: Starting a whole new life!

THESEUS: You may find Athens primitive after the glories
of Knossos.

ARIADNE: Wherever you are is Elysium to me.

THESEUS: *(getting uneasy)* My father Aegeus will be

charmed to meet you, I'm sure. Which reminds me. I must give the order to change the sails to white ones – to signal my father that I'm still alive.

(*He raises his hand to give the signal but is distracted by her next words*)

ARIADNE: Alive and coming home with your bride-to-be . . . Will he like me, do you suppose?

THESEUS: Bride?

ARIADNE: How soon can we be married, do you think? The first day? Or the second? Oh Theseus, I'm so happy!

ONE OF TRIBUTES: Land ho! Island off the starboard bow.

ARIADNE: Oh! Is that Athens?

THESEUS: No, no. That's Naxos. But we'll anchor there to take on water. Steersman, make for shore!

(*The 'ship' dismantles and* THESEUS *and* ARIADNE *settle down to sleep mid-stage*)

CHORUS: Happy Ariadne
Sleeps on the silk-soft sand.
Deeply she sleeps, and gladly,
Holding Theseus's hand.

(THESEUS *extricates himself and creeps away on exaggerated tiptoe, finger to lips, grinning. The others titter. Exit all but* ARIADNE, *asleep centre stage*)

Sleep on, Ariadne,
Poor, unlovely princess.
Some stories still end sadly
For girls who trust a promise.

ARIADNE: Theseus! I dreamed . . . Oh, Theseus! My love! Where are you? Are you hiding from me? Is it a game? Where is everybody? (*Seeing ship out in auditorium*) Theseus? Wait! You've forgotten me! Look! Here I am!

Don't go without me! For the sweet gods' sake, don't leave me here! Alone! Theseus!

(*She drops down in a crouch of despair.*

Enter AEGEUS *who goes to stand directly in front of her, at centre front of the stage. He too peers out to sea*)

CHORUS: It comes, not much belated,
Making his old eyes start:
The ship the King has awaited
With an aching, anxious heart.

AEGEUS: Oh, my son! Did you do it? Is it done? Is the Minotaur dead? Or did you . . . were you . . .

CHORUS: The bow-wave leaps with dolphins.
The sun is blinding bright.
The shriek of gulls engulfs him:
The sails are black as night.

AEGEUS: No! My son is dead! My son lies butchered in the Minotaur's lair. NO!

(*He leaps off the front of the stage*)

CHORUS: So hail the conquering hero
Who set Athenians free,
Who broke the neck of monsters
With borrowed trickery.
Who broke the heart of a maiden
And came home fancy free!
Your father lies full fathoms five
In the cold Aegean Sea.

(*Amid scenes of celebration,* THESEUS *is told the news of his father's death and stands looking shattered and aghast as the cast dance round him and away off stage*)

The Golden Apple

The world is becoming overcrowded, but Eris,
Goddess of Strife, has the solution in her pocket.
It is a golden apple.

Cast

ZEUS

HERMES

POSEIDON

ERIS

HERA

ATHENA

APHRODITE

PARIS, drawn from audience

Costumes

- gods as elsewhere
- earmuffs for Zeus
- gold band for Paris
- Eris needs a pocket, to hold the apple

Props

- Zeus's throne
- golden apple
- modelling balloon (optional, refers back to *The Race to Live*)
- 3 glove puppets: King, Prince, Princess

Special Effects

- sounds of battle
- swanee whistle (played live or recorded)
- 'Our 'Ermes' commentary could be pre-recorded; it is a parody of 'Our Graham' in *Blind Date* (as if you didn't know!)

Ideas!

This play deliberately slumps from comedy to tragedy. How are you going to get laughs and gulps in the right places?

What are the advantages and disadvantages of getting the audience involved?

THE GOLDEN APPLE

ZEUS, *wearing earmuffs, sits upstage left in his throne, silently fulminating. In one hand is a modelling balloon. He is in a filthy sulk.* HERMES *stands front left.*

(*Enter* POSEIDON *right, singing loudly*)

POSEIDON: Two men of Troy had two little toys;
One had a Wooden Horse! . . .

HERMES: Shshshsh! Zeus has a headache.

POSEIDON: Oh, no. Not another one. He's not expecting again, is he? Remember Athena?

(*He mimes headache, 'pulls open' his skull and lifts out something, sets it down and sidesteps into the space taking on a female stance*)

HERMES: No, no. It's just the noise.

POSEIDON: What noise?

HERMES: (*points into auditorium*) From down there.

POSEIDON: (*squinnies into auditorium*) Oh, them. I've got used to it. Besides, they're quite quiet tonight.

HERMES: But Zeus thinks there are too many of them. Always squabbling and singing and selling things to one another. He wants to *thin them out*.

POSEIDON: What, a sort of universal diet, you mean?

HERMES: No, no. Weed them out. (*Mimes weeding*)

POSEIDON: (*imitating mime*) Weeding . . . Ah! Weeding. I see. What does he have in mind, then? (*Raises hands above nose and eyes*) A flood? I could do him a tidal wave or two.

HERMES: Nah. Floods leave everything too damp.

POSEIDON: A plague, then?

HERMES: Nah. Plagues smell too bad.

POSEIDON: What, then? Target practice with the thunder-bolts?

> (*Both mime, starting to enjoy themselves*)

ZEUS: (*sitting bolt upright*) I've got it! Eris! Send for Eris! Send for the Goddess of Strife!

POSEIDON AND HERMES: (*looking at each other*) WAR!

> (*They exit, while* ERIS *enters and* ZEUS *whispers his instructions*)

ERIS: Understood, my Lord. I shall get on to it right away . . . Let me see. What shall it be? Ah yes! (*Taking golden apple from pocket*) There's the seed of it, your Majesty.

ZEUS: (*takes apple and examines it*) What's this written on it? 'For the Fairest'. (*Gives it back*) No. You've got me. How does it work?

> (*Enter* HERA, ATHENA *and* APHRODITE, *chattering good-naturedly*)

ERIS: Watch and see, my Lord. Watch and see.

> (*She leans down and bowls the apple among the 3 ladies' feet, then she and* ZEUS *hide behind the throne*)

HERA: (*picks up apple*) What's this? 'For the Fairest'. How nice. A present. For me.

APHRODITE: Oh, surely not! Not if it says 'For the Fairest'. Everyone knows that I . . .

ATHENA: It could have been meant for any one of us. I quite distinctly felt it brush my ankles. In fact I'm sure it was thrown directly in my path.

HERA: (*strident, à la Miss Piggy*) Zeus! Where are you, Zeus?

ZEUS: (*to* ERIS, *in hissed whisper, as they emerge from behind the throne*) I meant strife *on Earth*, you fool, not up here in Heaven!

ERIS: Aha! Watch and see, my Lord. Every War has to start with a quarrel.

ZEUS: (*to* HERA) You called, dearest?

HERA: Yes, Zeussy darling. This apple. Well, it fell. Sort of *in among us*, as it were. You didn't drop it, did you? With *me* in mind?

ATHENA: Right in my path, actually.

APHRODITE: But plainly meant for me.

HERA: And it says on it, 'For the Fairest'.

(*All three women strike beautiful poses*)

You see the problem. Perhaps you can say, dearest, which of us it was meant for?

ZEUS: I . . . ah . . . (*Gulps*)

ERIS: (*springs into action, efficient-secretary-style*) Oh, no, no, no, no, no, ladies. King Zeus is *far* too partial a judge. I mean to say, how is a god to choose between his wife and his daughters? Noo, noo, noo, noo, noooo! In fact it's *much* too hard a task for anyone on Olympus, ladies! What we need here is an impartial judge. (*Takes apple back*) Someone who has no axe to grind (so to speak), no reason to favour any one of you.

(*The three women regard* ERIS *coldly*)

Not me! Gracious, no! I was thinking perhaps of someone . . . *down there.*

> (*She points into the audience. The three regard her even
> more coolly*)

Not hoi polloi, naturally! Some king or prince. (*Knowingly*) Prince Paris, perhaps?

> (*All three melt, sigh and go moony*)

HERA/ATHENA/APHRODITE: Prince Paris!

ZEUS: Send for Prince Paris of . . . where?

HERA/ATHENA/APHRODITE: (*waspish*) Troy, of course!

ZEUS: Ah. Send for Prince Paris of Troy!

> (*When no one enters,* ALL *look out into the audience,
> shading eyes with their hands. An unsuspecting man is
> fetched from the front row – e.g. headmaster or care-
> taker – and drawn up onto the stage to sit in* ZEUS's
> throne. The GODDESSES *fuss round him, admiringly,
> besottedly*)

HERA: Now, Paris dear. Everyone knows you're a cultivated man with an eye for Beauty.

APHRODITE: Stop making up to him, Mother. Prince Paris is perfectly capable of deciding for himself . . . aren't you, you sweet—

ATHENA: (*barging them away from* PARIS) Give the poor man a chance to breathe!

ERIS: (*Scouse, Cilla Black impersonation*) The thing is, Prince Paris: a bit of a falling out's occurred, and we need someone to be judge. These three ladies—

> (*They cough at her, annoyed*)

—these three *eminencies* would like you to choose which of them is the rightful winner of this golden apple. (*Gives it to*

PARIS) Have a look-see, chuck. It's inscribed: 'For the Fairest'. So let me bring each of them to you in turn. (*Louche*) I am sure these luvly ladies will want to say a little *something* to you, to help you make up your mind.

(*As* HERA *approaches,* ERIS *steers* ATHENA *and* APHRODITE *away 'out of earshot'.* (POSEIDON *might engage them in conversation upstage right.*) ERIS *returns in 'beauty contest' mode, reading 'notes' from supposed filecards*)

Meet Hera, sir, Queen of the Gods, patron of marriage and children! Her ambition is 'to be a good wife and mother', and her hobbies are birdwatching and thwarting her husband . . . Won't you say a few words, your Majesty?

HERA: (*bossy*) Choose me, Paris, and I shall make you the most powerful ruler on any shore of the Central Sea! Africa, Crete, the Peloponnese . . . wherever you set foot, I shall have men bow down to you in homage. You shall be rich as Croesus: richer than Midas in his golden palace—

(ERIS *hustles her away and fetches* ATHENA)

ERIS: Athena, sir. Known to some as Pallas Athene and to her father as Little Grey Eyes. Goddess of battle, goddess of the city. Her hobbies are archery, weaving and virginity, and she would like to go on to be 'something in international diplomacy'. Tell us about yourself, Pallas . . .

(ERIS *steers* HERA *away out of earshot*)

ATHENA: Paris. How delightful to meet you at last. Call me Grey Eyes. (*Suddenly whispers, urgent and aggressive*) Choose me, Paris, and I shall give you victory in battle – conquest against every foe! Imagine the laurels circling your brow! Imagine the cheers of your troops! Picture banners flying over Troy as you march home after yet another bloody victory! (*Moving round behind throne and taking* PARIS *in a headlock*) Choose me, Prince Paris, and you won't be sorry.

ERIS: (*hastily returning*) Now, now. I hope you're not trying to influence the judge, Old Grey Eyes—

ATHENA: *Little* Grey Eyes!

ERIS: (*to* PARIS) And last but not least, I give you: Aphrodite. Goddess of . . . *Lerve*. Born from the sea foam! Serenaded by the dickie-birds. Wife of Hephaestus the Blacksmith.

(APHRODITE *shudders and glares*)

Not that she lets that hinder her.

(APHRODITE *kicks her in the shins*)

Adored by animals (and men) everywhere. Her hobbies are surfboarding and kissing, and her ambition is 'to help little children and bring peace and happiness wherever she goes'. Say a few words, won't you, Princess?

APHRODITE: (*vamps* PARIS *shamelessly*) Listen. Paris. Choose me and I shall give you the love of the most beautiful mortal woman in the world. Love absolute. Love everlasting. Love all-consuming. A love which the world will remember for a thousand years and more. What do you say?

(ERIS *flutters back to take charge, to the music of 'Blind Date' played on a swanee whistle*)

ERIS: Well, Prince Paris, you've met all three goddesses this evening and it's Make-Your-Mind-Up-Time. Here's Our 'Ermes to give you a helping hand.

HERMES: (*Louche*) There's Number One: she'd like to make you as rich and powerful as a celestial vindaloo! Then there's Number Two: she'd like to see you resting on your laurels, 'cos you just can't beat a *man in armour*!
And last but not least there's lovely Number Three. Well, she'd like to see you down in the Queen's Arms right after the show, because she's got *lerve* in mind.

ERIS: Thank you, Our 'Ermes. Now it's over to you, Prince Paris, you lucky man . . . The choice is a-a-a-a-ll YOURS!

(*More 'Blind Date' music on swanee whistle, ending in ugly downward slide. The protagonists freeze except for* ERIS, *who breaks off into her own character again, to address the audience. Complete change of mood*)

No choice at all, if we're honest. As I know, as Aphrodite knows, (*to audience*) as you all know: no man is going to choose fame or wealth over the love of the most beautiful woman in the world.

(APHRODITE *snatches the apple from* PARIS, *smiling smugly.* HERA *and* ATHENA *storm off right, complaining.* PARIS *is returned to his seat. Exit all but* HERMES *and* ERIS *who put on glove puppets – see below*)

The Golden Apple was awarded to Aphrodite – a toy – a bauble – a trophy. And Paris (*holds up glove puppet Prince, then Princess puppet*) was introduced to Helen: the most beautiful woman the world has ever seen. One look and he was stunned. One look and he was lost. So was she.

(*The puppets embrace.* HERMES *watches, stony-eyed*)

HERMES: Unfortunately, what Aphrodite had failed to mention was that Helen already had a husband (*holds up King puppet*) – King Menelaus of Sparta. Brother of King Agamemuch of Mycenae. The most powerful ruler among the city kingdoms. Paris and Helen eloped to Troy, saying how their love was fated – how the gods had meant them to be together: him and her, her and him.

(*Exit* ERIS, *with the Prince and Princess puppets 'eloping'*)

King Agamemnon's heart was broken. (*He punches his puppet hard in the chest, making it buckle over*) The shards flew out in all directions, slashing and maiming the Mediterranean world. Agamemnon mustered every ally – the best knights in his realm – anyone who had a score to settle with the Trojans – and he set sail for Troy. Even the gods took sides.

(*Rising noise of battle,* HERMES *shouts above it*)

For ten years the noise in Heaven was worse than ever. The clash of weapons, the neighing of horses, the rattle of chariots, the screams of the dying.

(*Noise dies away completely to silence.* HERMES *speaks in very deliberate, bitter, enunciated speech*)

But oh it was quiet afterwards.
So much more quiet.

(*Exit* HERMES)

Unbelievable Cassandra

Bad enough that Cassandra can see into the future. Worse still that no one believes what she can see.

Cast

CASSANDRA, Princess of Troy

at least 4 TROJAN SOLDIERS (no helmets)

PRIAM, King of Troy

HECUBA, Queen of Troy

MINISTER

TROJAN CHILD (POLITES)

APOLLO

POSEIDON

LAOCOON, a priest of Poseidon

4 GREEKS (the Trojans again but wearing Greek helmets)

Costumes

- gods as elsewhere
- crowns for Priam and Hecuba
- 4 Greek, face-concealing helmets (see illustration)
- an over-garment for Cassandra of thin, easily torn cloth, ready-nicked to assist tearing (a new one needed for each performance)
- priestly garb for Laocoon

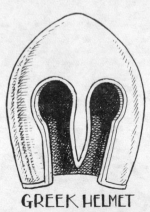

GREEK HELMET

Props

- 2 long ropes secured high up in the wings
- small mound of ashy dirt
- chess board and pieces
- small table
- 2 toy articulated snakes (sold as stocking-fillers)
- large, noisy triangle

Special Effects

- sound of hand-to-hand battle and raging fire
- orange and yellow travelling spotlights (optional)

Ideas!

Work out a Greek-style dance for when the Trojans celebrate the capture of the horse.

Have Cassandra circulate among the audience before the performance or during the interval, begging people not to go back to their seats for fear something terrible will happen.

Note

This is intended as a party piece for a *very* promising actress.

UNBELIEVABLE CASSANDRA

2 long ropes are fastened at one end high up in the right-hand wings but as yet hang down offstage. PRINCESS CASSANDRA, *daughter of* KING PRIAM *of Troy, sits cross-legged near the stage front. There is a small pile of ashy dirt in front of her. On the other side of the stage,* APOLLO *and* POSEIDON *are playing chess at a small table. (Ideally they should be raised high up above the stage, but this is probably not practical/safe)*

CASSANDRA: I'm not mad. People say I'm mad, but I'm not mad. Not yet, anyway. That's still to come. Inside my head, the kindling's already there. Sharp sticks. Thorny sticks. And the pictures come drifting downwind, like burning embers off a bonfire. Into my head . . . My dreams are already full of fire. My ears are full of screaming. I can smell the smoke just as if it was in my nostrils. What do you think it's like, seeing into the future? Like watching fish from a river bank? That's not how it is. It's like having your whole head pushed underwater, and the fish are swimming through your brain. Fish. And monsters. And worse.

(Enter 2 TROJANS, *one excitably pointing back off stage at something he has seen)*

TROJAN 1: They are! They're packing up, I tell you! They're striking camp! Go and see for yourself if you don't believe me!

TROJAN 2: Nah. Why should they leave now? They're still revelling in killing Prince Hector.

TROJAN 1: They lost Achilles – their greatest champion. Maybe it's made them lose heart.

CASSANDRA: So. It's beginning. The end is beginning. (*To* TROJAN 1) Is there a horse? Some kind of a horse?

TROJAN 1: (*to* TROJAN 2, *as if he has not heard*) And there's this horse! Giant wooden horse!

CASSANDRA: There you are! I told you! In my visions I saw a horse!

TROJAN 1: (*with contempt*) You just heard me say it. That's not fortune-telling; that's eavesdropping.

CASSANDRA: But you don't understand. I knew! I saw it in my head! And it's not just a model. It's hollow. They are going to hide soldiers inside it!

TROJAN 2: You been out there, have you? When was that, then?

(*The two turn their backs to exclude* CASSANDRA *from their conversation but she dodges round them, plucking at their clothes*)

What do you think it is, then, this horse? Some kind of monument to their fallen heroes?

(TROJAN 1 *goes to hit* CASSANDRA, *but* TROJAN 2 *stops him*)

Steady. She is the King's daughter . . . whatever else she is.

(*They go off stage to get away from her*)

CASSANDRA: (*calling after them*) You've got to listen! Why don't you listen! It's hollow! The horse is hollow!

(*She freezes.* APOLLO *laughs loudly, unkindly*)

POSEIDON: What's so funny?

APOLLO: That crazy-woman.

POSEIDON: The Princess Cassandra? I thought you were . . . well, you know . . . *involved*, the two of you.

APOLLO: Oh I . . . er . . . smelled the roses for a while. But you know how it is. Stay too long and the roses start to twine themselves around your neck.

(*They go back to playing chess. Enter* KING PRIAM *and his wife* HECUBA)

CASSANDRA: Father! Oh, Father, please listen to me! You've got to listen!

PRIAM: (*uneasy*) Oh. Good day to you, Cassandra. Are you feeling any . . . easier in your mind?

HECUBA: Cassandra, dear, your father is very busy. Affairs of state. The war.

CASSANDRA: But it's about the war! It's about the horse on the beach! You mustn't fetch it inside the city, Father. Whatever you do, don't fetch it in!

PRIAM: Apparently it is some kind of tribute – either to Poseidon and his sea horses, or to Troy, the City of the Horse.

CASSANDRA: It's neither, Father. It's a trick! Odysseus the Cunning thought of it. It's a trick to get inside the city. You've got to believe me!

HECUBA: (*sharply*) Cassandra. Have you nothing better to do? It is hardly seemly for a Princess of Troy to run around the streets making a spectacle of herself.

CASSANDRA: Be quiet, Mother! Be quiet and listen! You wouldn't listen when I warned you all those years ago – about Paris stealing another man's wife! I warned you about the war – that it would mean the end for Troy. I told you then: we're all going to die, Mother! That horse out there . . .

HECUBA: (*squeamish and prim*) And so gloomy always. This really doesn't help the war effort, you know, Cassandra.

(*The action freezes*)

POSEIDON: (*with sudden insight*) She turned you down, didn't she? Cassandra turned you down!

APOLLO: Rubbish. I just . . . tired of her.

POSEIDON: (*hugely amused*) No, no, I see it all now! You fell in love with her – gave her the power of prophecy – but she wasn't interested, am I right? I'm right, aren't I? She probably looked into the future and saw what a fly-by-night you'd be! So she turned you down!

APOLLO: I am a god – an Olympian. I can have any woman who takes my fancy.

POSEIDON: (*laughing*) She did! She turned you down!

APOLLO: It's your move. Are we playing or what?

(*They return to their game of chess. Enter a* MINISTER *reporting to* PRIAM)

PRIAM: I can hardly believe it is all over! But the beach out there really is empty. The siege is lifted. The Greeks have sailed away. Just one slave-boy left sitting in the shade of a great wooden horse.

MINISTER: His name is Sinon, your Highness. He says that the horse is an offering to the gods, in return for a safe journey home. Haha! How that boy hates the Greeks! You should hear the names he was calling them!

CASSANDRA: A very convincing liar.

MINISTER: The slave boy says: capture that horse and we will have taken prisoner the veritable spirit of Athens!

CASSANDRA: If it's the spirit of Athens, set it alight – why not? – and watch it burn!

PRIAM: Give word for the horse to be hauled inside the city on ropes.

(*Exit* MINISTER. PRIAM *goes off with* HECUBA, *saying to her*)

Can't something be done about Cassandra? She's clearly not well.

CASSANDRA: No, no, no! Why won't you believe me!? It's like being invisible! It's like being underwater. I scream and no one hears me.

POSEIDON: So you cursed her, didn't you? That's it! You put a curse on her.

APOLLO: Me? I gave her the gift of prophecy.

POSEIDON: Yes, but she wasn't sufficiently grateful, was she?

CASSANDRA: One kiss, he said. One kiss and I'll go, if that's what you truly want. (*With* APOLLO, *in unison*) One kiss.

APOLLO: (*continuing without break*) And I breathed into her the power to see what the future held in store.

CASSANDRA/APOLLO: (*in unison*) One kiss.

APOLLO: (*continuing without break*) And I sucked out of her the ring of truth.

POSEIDON: Now, whatever she says, no one believes her.

APOLLO: Not a soul.

CASSANDRA: I'm invisible. I'm inside a sealed jar, screaming. (*Shouts at audience; blinkers her eyes to show she is foreseeing the future*) TROY IS GOING TO BURN! CAN'T YOU SMELL THE SMOKE? CAN'T YOU HEAR THE SCREAMING? YOU ARE GOING TO DIE – AND YOU – AND YOU – AND YOU – AND

YOU. And I'm running through streets full of burning rubble, with Greek soldiers snatching at my hair and clothes, and sniggering: 'What a beauty – she's mine!' But I've run into the Temple of Athena, and I'm clinging to the statue of the goddess, begging her to save me. But they just break down the door, plank by plank, laughing, jeering . . . And now they're prising my fingers from round the statue – smashing at my hands with their sword hilts, dragging me outside . . .

(*She sinks down to the floor and curls up in a ball. Enter* LAOCOON, *passing close in front of her. She grabs hold of his ankles*)

Please! Listen! The wooden horse is a trick! There are men hiding inside it – Greeks – Odysseus the Cunning and a dozen more. And we're going to fetch them inside the city! We mustn't! It would be like giving them a key, saying, 'Come in! Come and murder us in our beds!'

LAOCOON: Hmmm. You could be right. I do not trust the Greeks, even when they do come bearing gifts.

CASSANDRA: You believe me?

(APOLLO *and* POSEIDON *have both stood up, startled*)

APOLLO: Who *is* this?

POSEIDON: That's Laocoon. One of my priests. Perhaps he is immune to you magic. Or maybe he just has more common sense than the rest.

APOLLO: (*spoiled whine*) But he'll spoil everything.

(TROJANS *enter 'pulling' on the two ropes. By letting the ropes slide through their hands, they appear to make progress in dragging something almost on stage.* CASSANDRA *tries to prise their fingers off the ropes and is pushed aside time and again*)

CASSANDRA: Don't! Please! Stop! Leave it outside! The horse is full of Greek soldiers! Look! There'll be a trap door. They'll come out tonight and unlock the gates. The Greeks are coming back! They'll stab you in your beds! They'll torch the city!

(*She is knocked over by the dancing which sponta-neously breaks out among the* TROJANS. *They gradu-ally break off and listen as* LAOCOON *begins to speak*)

LAOCOON: (*calm and rational*) One moment. I understand your glee – your relief. Myself, I'm sick to my soul with this war. But think. The Greeks pride themselves on their trickery. Might this horse not be a trick? Would it not be better to burn it, than fetch it into the very heart of our city?

TROJAN 1: Burn it? But it's our trophy!

TROJAN 2: We should deck it with flowers!

TROJAN 3: And dance round it!

LAOCOON: But first leave it outside. Just for a day. Ten years the wars have dragged on. Ten years we have waited for an end to the killing. Is it too much to wait one more day? I and my sons will go down to the shore and make sacrifice to Poseidon. He will reveal the truth to me, his priest.

CASSANDRA: At last! An ally! Someone who believes me!

(*Exit* LAOCOON. *The* TROJANS *call after him*)

TROJAN 3: You'll see! There's nothing out there now but the ashes of a thousand campfires.

TROJAN 2: The Greeks are gone!

APOLLO: (*to* POSEIDON) Well? He's your priest. What are you going to do? You and I, we built the walls of Troy for these people – sullied our hands . . .

POSEIDON: I didn't notice you sullying your hands. You just stood by and played your lyre.

APOLLO: And then the King refused to pay us. Isn't that right? He wouldn't pay us for our hard labour? That was when we sided with the Greeks. So are you going to let this . . . this *priest* thwart them?

POSEIDON: (*wearily*) Apollo, you have all the pity of a black widow spider.

(*He takes out 2 toy hinged snakes and makes them wriggle in mid-air*)

CASSANDRA: (*back on her spot by the ash-pile, hands blinkering her eyes as before*) Oh no! Oh you gods! Laocoon, COME BACK! Don't go down to the shore! I've seen what's going to happen! No! No! NO! *NO!* Be like the rest! Call me a madwoman like the rest! Anything! But don't go down to the beach! STOP HIM! MAKE HIM BELIEVE YOU! GODS! GODS! MAKE HIM BELIEVE THE OTHERS, NOT ME!

(*Enter* TROJAN 4, *looking sickened and pointing back
into the wings*)

TROJAN 4: Did you see? It was terrible! That old priest
Laocoon and his little boys . . . They were praying down on
the shore, and these *things* . . . sea snakes – huge – gigantic
– immense snakes came out of the surf—

(*People make as if to go and help*)

It's too late. It's no good. They're gone. Laocoon. The little
boys. Crushed. Swallowed up.

CASSANDRA: (*sinking back onto her spot*) Like litter
washed off the beach by an outgoing tide.

TROJAN 1: It's a sign. He doubted.

TROJAN 2: He wanted to burn the wooden horse.

TROJAN 3: But the gods wanted us to have it.

TROJAN 4: They didn't want us to doubt.

TROJAN 1: Zeus sent those snakes, that's what.

HECUBA: Gather flowers to decorate the horse.

CHILD [POLITES]: Can I go with them, Mother? Can I
really go outside and pick flowers?

HECUBA: Yes, child. Go outside. The siege is lifted. The
Greeks have gone. Ten years of war are over, thanks be to
the gods!

(*Exit* CHILD, POSEIDON *and* TROJAN 4, *taking chess
board and table with them.* APOLLO *remains, leaning
against the proscenium, smugly gloating*)

CASSANDRA: (*cross-legged, picking up ash and rubbing it
into her hair*) Over. Yes. Ten years of war. Tonight.
Tonight every Trojan man and boy will be put to the
sword.

TROJAN 1: She's stark mad, you know.

(*Exit* TROJAN 1)

CASSANDRA: Every woman and girl taken into slavery.

TROJAN 2: Sad. Probably the death of her brothers turned her brain.

(*Exit* TROJAN 2)

CASSANDRA: They will even slaughter the pigs in their sties. (*Makes squealing noises*)

TROJAN 3: Listen to that. Night and morning. Meaningless babbling.

(*Exit* TROJAN 3)

CASSANDRA: The fires will burn so bright that sailors ten miles out at sea will mistake them for beacons. The smoke will choke out the moon.

HECUBA: Is this any way for a Princess of Troy to behave? Get up. Go indoors. I've lost all patience with you.

(*Exit* HECUBA)

CASSANDRA: My father. My mother. My little brother. All my kin. All hacked down like briars. And you.

PRIAM: (*offering a hand*) Daughter. Cassandra. Won't you come in?

(*She ignores him. Exit* PRIAM)

CASSANDRA: (*rending her clothes once with each sentence; level, reasoned speech*) Even now, the Greek fleet is sailing back over the horizon. Tonight the trap-door will open in the belly of that horse, and down they'll climb – Odysseus and his men – stretching their cramped legs. They'll open the city gate and let in the enemy—

(GREEKS *tiptoe across back of stage*)

setting light to roof thatches, reaching in through windows to steal little trinkets. Souvenirs.

(*A big triangle clangs in alarum*)

Eventually someone will sound the alarm bell and our men will stumble out of doors still drunk from celebrating, sandals in their hands, and die barefoot.

(*If possible, orange and yellow lights whirl and cross, also sound effects, giving an impression of fire and battle*)

Apollo, I'm sorry! I'm yours if you want me! I'm sorry I spurned you! Lift the curse! Let them believe me! I'll be anything you like! I'll love you for ever!

APOLLO: (*extreme disgust*) You? Look at you. What would I want with a *madwoman*?

CASSANDRA: (*spitting at him*) A curse on you, then, Apollo! May there come a day when the whole world sees through you to what you are. Better! When the whole world doesn't even BELIEVE YOU EXIST! (*Startled, she blinkers her eyes once more*) Oh! I see it! I see it coming! It *will* come! (*She laughs*)

(CASSANDRA *continues to sit rocking to and fro. Enter* 2 GREEKS. APOLLO *points her out to them*)

GREEK 1: What a beauty – she's mine!

(CASSANDRA *jumps to her feet and runs off, pursued by the* GREEKS. *The noise of battle and fire builds up to a cacophony*)

Uphill Struggle

As Sisyphus discovers: you can fool the gods
once, but when they catch up with you, there is
hell to pay.

Cast

SISYPHUS

MEROPE

PLUTO

PERSEPHONE

THANATOS (Death)

various SPIRITS OF THE UNDERWORLD

2 NEIGHBOURS

Costumes

- Pluto and Persephone as elsewhere
- gauzy grey scarves for the Dead

Props

- dummy dressed like Sisyphus
- 2 thrones
- toy periscope
- small tatty suitcase
- large boulder made of chicken-wire and papier mâché

Special Effects

- amplified booming voice for Pluto's opening speeches

Idea!

One group might like to devise a brief scene representing the torment of Tantalus who was punished by Pluto with a raging thirst and ravening hunger while cool water flowed by and fruit dangled just out of his reach; also a huge rock hovered over his head threatening to crush him. This 'extra' could even be inserted into the play.

UPHILL STRUGGLE

PLUTO *and* PERSEPHONE *sit throned at the back of the stage. Nearby stands* THANATOS *holding a toy periscope. At the front of the stage,* SISYPHUS *lies under a blanket,* MEROPE *kneeling behind him, face-in-hands. Between them, hidden by the blanket, is a cloth dummy dressed like* SISYPHUS.

(*A big, hollow, booming voice echoes around the stage, while* PLUTO *mimes*)

PLUTO: Sisyphus! Sisyphus! It is time!

SISYPHUS: It's time, wife! I hear the summons! Pluto is calling me! I've got to go. Down to the Underworld. Out of the sunlight. Remember, won't you? Remember!

MEROPE: Oh, but Sisyphus!

SISYPHUS: Remember – just remember to do as I said. All will be well. All will be—

PLUTO: SISYPHUS!

(SISYPHUS *'dies', gets up and is escorted around the stage by* SPIRITS *draped in grey-gauze scarves. He too is given a scarf, frisked by* THANATOS, *then brought before* PLUTO's *throne.*

Meanwhile MEROPE *jumps up, gleefully, and toes the dummy 'body' with one foot*)

MEROPE: Dead! (*Kicks the dummy*) Dead and gone! (*Jumps on body with both feet*) Come and see, everybody! That great lummock of a husband of mine has slipped his moorings!

(*Enter* 2 NEIGHBOURS)

NEIGHBOUR 1: Sisyphus is dead?

MEROPE: Yep!

NEIGHBOUR 2: Dead, as in 'passed over'?

MEROPE: Dead as in 'defunct'. Snuffed out. Kicked the bucket. Popped his pattens. Croaked. Turned up his toes. (*Kicks the dummy again*)

NEIGHBOUR 1: We're very sorry to hear that, Merope. You were so . . .

MEROPE: Good riddance to bad rubbish, I say! Never liked him, and now I'm free of him! (*Pulls faces at the dummy*)

NEIGHBOUR 2: When's the funeral? I'll cook something. Baked meats. Something.

MEROPE: Funeral? Waste of money! I'd sooner spend it on a party. Just give me a hand to throw this trash on the compost heap.

NEIGHBOURS: Oh, but Merope . . . !

MEROPE: What? Oh, it's all right. He didn't die of anything contagious. Come on. Lend me a hand. He'll be in his natural element among the rhubarb leaves.

(*They swing the dummy head-and-heels, and throw it off stage.* MEROPE *brushes the palms of her hands together, dances a jig, then runs off stage*)

NEIGHBOUR 1: (*to other* NEIGHBOUR) She threw her husband on the rubbish dump!

NEIGHBOUR 2: (*to audience*) She danced on his memory.

NEIGHBOUR 1: Shocking!

NEIGHBOUR 2: Unheard of!

NEIGHBOUR 1: Has she no shame?

NEIGHBOUR 2: (*in going*) And I always thought those two were so close.

(*Exit both* NEIGHBOURS)

PLUTO: Speak, mortal . . . but I am warning you. I never yet heard an excuse good enough for a man to leave here and return to the Overworld.

SISYPHUS: It's my wife.

PERSEPHONE: (*gently, sympathetically*) She will manage, you know. People do. She will grieve for a time, but then—

SISYPHUS: But that's just it, madam! She isn't grieving at all! Merope is dancing and singing and throwing a party for everyone in the street!! She has given my body no funeral rites – just thrown me onto the compost heap like an old geranium!

PLUTO: No!

PERSEPHONE: How dreadful!

PLUTO: Is this true, Thanatos?

(THANATOS *holds up his periscope as if scanning the Overworld*)

THANATOS: Checking, your Majesty.

PERSEPHONE: Oh, you poor soul!

PLUTO: Even the most loveless widow usually puts on some show of grief for appearances' sake. What do you see, Thanatos?

THANATOS: Balloons and bunting. There's a band . . . and dancing. Retsina. The smashing of plates.

PLUTO: Shameful!

PERSEPHONE: What an unspeakable lady!

SISYPHUS: Imagine her face if I were to turn up at that

party, Lord Pluto. I'd chill the blood in her veins. I'd stand the hair clean up on her head. I'd send her scurrying to your temple on her knees to beg forgiveness.

THANATOS: (*still looking through periscope*) Bouzouki music.

PLUTO: She certainly deserves to be shocked out of this sacrilege . . .

THANATOS: Baklava cake!

SISYPHUS: And I'd come straight back, of course. One quick visit, that's all it would take.

THANATOS: Olives on sticks!

PERSEPHONE: Do let him go, Pluto! This wife of his is unnatural! She ought to be punished!

THANATOS: Squid nibbles!

PLUTO: (*his mind made up by the squid*) *Squid nibbles?!* Very well! Go, Sisyphus! Go back and teach your shameless wife some respect for the Dead! You have until tomorrow noon.

SISYPHUS: (*bowing deeply*) I thank you, most just and powerful Pluto. By noon tomorrow I shall return.

(*He heads back the way he has come, flinging aside his grey scarf.* MEROPE, *meanwhile, hurries on stage with a small suitcase and mimes packing. From opposite sides of the stage they see one another.* MEROPE *runs to* SISYPHUS *and they hug ecstatically*)

MEROPE: Sisyphus!

SISYPHUS: Let me look at you.

MEROPE: Oh, I've missed you so much!

SISYPHUS: Didn't I say it would work? Didn't I tell you I could trick my way out of the Underworld? All the powers of Hell couldn't part you and me, Merope. Beloved Merope . . . Are you ready?

MEROPE: Yes, yes. I've packed everything we need. It isn't much.

(*She fastens the case and they slip away off front of stage and down the centre of the auditorium, speaking as they go*)

SISYPHUS: We can walk as far as the harbour and take a boat out to the islands. We'll find somewhere so small – so out of the way – that no one will find us in a hundred years!

MEROPE: But what will Pluto do when you don't go back?

SISYPHUS: Accch. What's one soul among a hundred thousand? He'll never miss me . . . Or if he does, we'll be far away. His henchmen will never find me. Come on!

(*Exit* SISYPHUS *and* MEROPE, *from back of hall,
provided they can reach the wings again quickly from
there*)

PLUTO: Tell me, Thanatos, where is Sisyphus? Is he on his
way back?

THANATOS: (*scans with periscope through 360°*) I see him.
He is lying in a hammock on a beach. His wife is slicing a
pomegranate. The juice runs between her fingers. (*Everybody on stage groans yearningly*) Now and then, she slips a
seed between his lips.

(PLUTO *and* PERSEPHONE *look at one another and she
covers his hand with hers*)

There is a baby playing in the sand.

PERSEPHONE: I *knew* there couldn't really be a woman as
wicked as Sisyphus said.

PLUTO: Does he really think he can escape me that easily?
Doesn't he know what I'll do to him when finally I reef him
in?

PERSEPHONE: Perhaps he thought it was worth it . . .

THANATOS: . . . for a few more days with his wife.

PLUTO: (*stands up and bellows*) SUMMON SISYPHUS!!

(*All on stage pass the words around in a hissing
whisper: 'Summon Sisyphus', 'Summon Sisyphus'.*
SISYPHUS *is flung on stage and sprawls at* PLUTO's *feet.
He is wearing a scarf again.* MEROPE *follows after a
time, also with scarf*)

PLUTO: (*working himself up to a rage*) Oh accursed,
wicked Sisyphus! Did you really think to trick your way
into immortality? Did you really suppose you could break
your word to a god and escape retribution?

SISYPHUS: Well, begging your pardon, Mightiness, but

what did I have to lose? (*To audience*) What reward can we Greeks earn by perfect obedience, eh? Good and bad, we all come here in the end – to this half-light half-life. Well, on Earth I was that most admired of men – the best thing a Greek could be – a *trickster*. (*To* PLUTO) I may have broken faith with you, your Lowness, you Ruler of Darkness, you Keeper of Gloom . . . but I was true to myself. With deepest respect, sir, you take your eyes off me and I'll be gone again in a flash. On that you have my word.

PLUTO: (*appears to think this over*) Very well.

(*He snaps his fingers and the* SPIRITS *roll on stage a large boulder, and form themselves into a slope – see illustration*)

Roll this boulder to the very top of the slope and you are free to go, Sisyphus. You and your wife.

(SISYPHUS *tries. Boulder tumbles back from the top to the bottom. He tries again.* MEROPE *helps him*)

When I am done with you, Sisyphus, you will be too weary to go anywhere. You will crave rest. You will crave the shadowy nothingness of these floating spirits. I have devised a punishment for you which will keep you labouring till the Crack of Doom! Now curse me, if you have the breath. Curse me and be sorry!

SISYPHUS: (*heaving and straining as he speaks*) Curse you, Pluto? I don't curse you. I thank you! Thanks to you, I am not like these others here. Not like them, and not like you. I have HOPE, Pluto. Something to look forward to! Even if I push this boulder a million times up the hill . . . and watch it roll back down a million times—

PLUTO: Oh you will, Sisyphus, you will!

SISYPHUS: —still I shall always have the *possibility* of succeeding – of going back into the sunlight. And that's more than even you can hope for. Isn't it?

THANATOS: (*after looking through periscope*) And up in the sunlit world, Sisyphus has another consolation. A son. A trickster just like his father. Probably the greatest, most revered trickster of all. Even now, while Sisyphus toils on and on, perpetually rolling his boulder up the hill of Eternity and watching it roll back down, mortals high above his head tell and retell stories about his famous trickster son: ODYSSEUS!

(*Exit* ALL)

Odysseus and the Sirens

Just one adventure of many . . .

Cast

HERMES

ODYSSEUS

CIRCE

3 SIRENS (who also play SCYLLA)

EURYLOCHOS, second-in-command to Odysseus

7 other ROWERS (variable)

POSEIDON

Costumes

- Poseidon and Hermes as elsewhere
- blank white masks for Sirens
- hag masks for Sirens
- magician's cloak for Circe (optional)
- Captain's cap to mark out Odysseus

Props

- round shields for the crew
- snake-head glove puppets for Sirens (the size of oven gloves)
- rope (optional)
- a stake/mast
- blown-up clip-sealed or self-seal balloons (extra big)

Special Effects

- pre-recorded Siren Song, scream, storm at sea; possibly even the noise of rowing

Ideas!

Have fun pre-recording the Siren Song: a mixture of weird, wailing noises and garbled, meaningless words.

Decorate cardboard shields with popular Greek symbols – Greek key, monsters etc.

ODYSSEUS AND THE SIRENS

At the rear of the stage sit the SIRENS, *intertwined at the legs, facing the audience. They wear blank white masks over their faces and ugly masks (unseen as yet) on the backs of their heads. On their hands are gloves like snake-heads – the heads of* SCYLLA.

(*Enter* ODYSSEUS *raised shoulder high amid cheering* CREW)

HERMES: Odysseus. Hero of Troy. His idea it was to build the Wooden Horse which fooled the Trojans. He it was who set sail for Ithaca, after ten years of war, with twelve ships full of men, and braved the giants of Laestrygonia . . .

(ODYSSEUS *and* CREW *look up, scream and run off other side of stage. In the wings they snatch up a stake and . . .*)

. . . blinded the one-eyed Cyclops called Polyphemus . . .

(. . . *charge across the stage with it, roaring, straight into the opposite wings. Sound effect of horrible scream. The men re-enter, picking their way cautiously right across the stage, looking around them in horror*)

. . . visited the Underworld itself . . .

CREW: Oooooooer. Urgch. Eeek.

HERMES: . . . took possession of the very winds of the sea! . . .

(*Blown-up balloons are thrust into the hands of the* CREW, *out of the wings. They immediately let go of them and let them spurt and blart off around stage*)

(*disgustedly*) and let them loose.

Odysseus it was who fought with the vile Scylla . . .

(ODYSSEUS *goes to the writhing* SCYLLA, *pulls its snakehead gloves off one by one and throws them into the wings. Exit* ODYSSEUS *into wings*)

. . . who braved the whirlpool Charybdis . . .

(*The* CREW *form themselves into a circle and, holding hands, start to whirl faster and faster. Dizzy, they break away, stumble and fall down on all fours. Re-enter* ODYSSEUS *from wings holding* CIRCE *round the throat*)

. . . and saved his men from the pigsty of the sorceress Circe, who had turned them all into swine.

CREW: (*to audience*) Oink Oink.

(*The 'pigs' crawl off stage and collect their round shields*)

HERMES: But listen! and I will tell you how Odysseus heard the music of the Sirens and lived to tell the tale!

(CIRCE'*s wrestling match with* ODYSSEUS *turns into an embrace. They walk around the stage, his arm around her*)

CIRCE: Must you go, Odysseus? All my life I waited for you to fulfil the prophecy and stifle my magic with love. And now are you really going to leave me?

ODYSSEUS: I have frittered away a year already. On Ithaca, my wife Penelope is waiting, besieged by men telling her I am dead, telling her to remarry. I am King of Ithaca, and Ithaca needs its King.

CIRCE: Go then, but if you want to reach home alive, beware the Sirens. They have been the undoing of better sailors than you.

ODYSSEUS: What is so dangerous about them? Are they like the Lotus Eaters? Do they tempt a man into a life of idleness? I soon put paid to the Lotus Eaters.

CIRCE: No, no. The Sirens are far harder to resist. It's their singing, you see. Oh, their singing!

(*Siren Song – quiet, weird music mixed with garbled singing. The* SIRENS *beckon to the audience and move their mouths. Fades*)

It lures men to their deaths. Don't deceive yourself, my love. I can read your thoughts. 'They wouldn't get the better of Odysseus,' you are telling yourself. 'I could resist them.' But you couldn't. Not even you. No one ever has. The Sirens are not just musical – they are magical. Here, then. Here's wax – soft beeswax. Plug your ears and the ears of your crew. And do it before the music comes to you over the water – before you hear the first note. Or you'll never see Ithaca or that wife of yours again!

(*The* CREW *line up and sit down, holding their round shields to represent the sides of the boat. They are rowers now. The stake represents the mast, supported by 2 of the* CREW. ODYSSEUS *steps into the boat and waves goodbye to* CIRCE. *The* CREW *mime rowing.* CIRCE *turns away, shaking her head dismally. Exit* CIRCE)

ALL ROWERS: Into the wine-dark sea we dip our oars,
Thinking of dear ones left on distant shores;
Heaving with all our might against the sea
Whose angry master mutters vengefully.
Spare us, waves! Oh spare us, cruel sea!
To see the end of this, our Odyssey!

Spare us, waves! Oh spare us, cruel sea!
To see the end of this, our Odyssey!

ODYSSEUS: Listen, men! Within a league or two, we shall
sail by the lair of the Sirens. Don't remove this wax from
your ears whatever happens.

(*He passes down the 'boat', miming stopping ears,*
except for EURYLOCHUS*'s*)

Now, Eurylochus, bind me to the mast and, whatever I say,
ignore me until the island is past and out of sight.

EURYLOCHUS: Bind you, Captain? (*He does so*)

ROWER 1: There he goes again: Odysseus.

ROWER 2: Going one better than the rest of us.

ROWER 3: Always the exception to the rules.

ROWER 4: He the clever one and we the fools.

EURYLOCHUS: (*to* ODYSSEUS) You heard Circe. Surely
you don't mean to listen to the Siren Song? It may strike you
dead like a bolt of lightning!

ODYSSEUS: It might. But where's the victory in *not* doing,
in *not* hearing, in *not* finding out? How could I tell my
grandchildren that I escaped the Sirens and not be able to
tell them what I escaped? Use your best knots, now.

EURYLOCHUS: Some of us would settle for just *seeing* our
grandchildren.

ODYSSEUS: Then get back to your oar, stop up your ears,
and don't stop rowing, no matter what.

(*The* CREW *mime rowing. Enter* POSEIDON)

POSEIDON: So! You dare to venture out again across the
glass roof of my palace, do you, Odysseus? You who step
from adventure to adventure using the faces of others for
stepping stones. My poor blind son, the Cyclops. Poor

broken-hearted Circe. The crews of the eleven ships which sank in your wake. Step carefully, Odysseus. One slip and I will have you.

(*Exit* POSEIDON.

The Siren Song starts – must not be so loud that it drowns ODYSSEUS*'s words. The* SIRENS *sway in time to the music*)

ODYSSEUS: Oh! The music! Listen to the music! Circe lied! They're not witches at all! They're just young girls marooned here by her filthy magic! Listen, men! Oh, you fools, take the wax out of your ears and listen! They know our names! They have heard of me! They say they've been waiting for me all this time! Right through the War. Right through our voyaging! Pull for the shore, men! We can find room for them between our feet! Do as you are told! I gave you a direct command!

How beautiful they are! Such pleading in their eyes! Such sadness in their mouths! Oh, *this* is why the gods sent me this way! They wanted me to help these poor young things. Oh, that music! It melts my soul like ice in hot wine.

Untie me, Eurylochus! Do you dare disobey a direct order? Never mind what I said before. I am commanding you to untie me. Take the wax out of your ears, you fools, and row for the island! Look! Are you blind as well as deaf? We can provision the boat there! There are fruit trees, beaches, landing places! Row for the shore, you dolts, or, so help me, when I get free I'll throw every disobedient mutineer overboard with my own hands! Numbskulls! Morons! Look how they weep to see us row past! Haven't you got one drop of pity in your scurvy souls? How can you desert them? Look! Look!

All right, all right, have it your way, you mindless dogs! Let me go to them at least. Cut me loose and I'll swim over to them – it isn't far. Eurylochus, do it! You can read my lips, I know. Obey me or you are finished as my second-in-command. *Take the wax out of your ears, will you? For the gods' sake! LET ME GO! I SHALL DIE IF I DON'T GO TO THEM!*

(*He slumps miserably in his ropes. Siren Song fades. The* SIRENS *freeze. The* MEN *look over their shoulders and 'rest on their oars'.* EURYLOCHUS *indicates they should remove the wax, does so himself, then gets up and goes to untie* ODYSSEUS)

EURYLOCHUS: Look. You've chafed all the skin off your wrists, Captain.

ODYSSEUS: What did you see, Eurylochus? Tell me what you saw.

EURYLOCHUS: A heap of rocks jagged as broken glass.

ROWER 1: Heaped with the hulks of a hundred ships.

ROWER 2: White with the bones of countless sailors.

ROWER 3: And the stench!

(*They all gag*)

ROWER 4: And those ugly hags! More grotesque even than the rotting skulls.

(*The* SIRENS *turn their backs to display hag masks on the backs of their heads*)

ROWER 5: Gnashing their teeth as if they were eating us already.

ROWER 6: It could have been us.

ROWER 7: It should have been us.

EURYLOCHUS: Praise the gods for the sorceress Circe!

ALL ROWERS: Praise the gods for wise Circe!

ODYSSEUS: Praise the gods for Circe.

EURYLOCHUS: Still. Something to tell your grandchildren, Captain, eh?

ODYSSEUS: I— Yes, yes! (*Recovering himself*) I shall tell them how I, King Odysseus, tricked the Sirens out of their prey and I'll sing them a snatch of the Siren Song . . . (*He tries to, but cannot*) That's odd. It's gone. I can't call it to mind. Too strange. Too slippery to hold on to . . .

EURYLOCHUS: Me, I shall tell my grandchildren to stay on dry land and never to venture out to sea.

ROWER 1: That's if our grandchildren remember us when we get home.

ROWER 2: That's if we ever get home.

ODYSSEUS: (*oblivious to their comments*) Lean on your oars, men! Look to your oars! We've heard the Sirens and lived!

ROWER 3: That's the difference between him and us.

ROWER 4: We've seen the Sirens and part of us has died.

ROWER 5: He remembers the triumph and the music.

ROWER 6: Our memories are all back there, among the bones and the stink.

ALL ROWERS: Into the wine-dark sea we dip our oars,
Thinking of dear ones left on distant shores;
Spare us, waves! Oh spare us, cruel sea!
To see the end of this, our Odyssey!
Spare us, waves! Oh spare us, cruel sea!
To see the end of this, our Odyssey!

(They 'row' off stage. POSEIDON *steps on from the other side and conjures a storm. Pre-recorded sounds of storm at sea)*

Riddle of the Sphinx

What has four legs in the morning, two in the afternoon and three in the evening . . . and why is it a matter of life and death?

Cast

QUIZMASTER

CONTESTANTS: RED
                      BLUE
                      GREEN
                      YELLOW
                      NEW YELLOW

PRIME MINISTER

QUEEN JOCASTA

OEDIPUS

THE SPHINX

Costumes

- team bands for contestants
- crown for Queen Jocasta
- chain of office for Prime Minister
- glitzy jacket for quizmaster
- one big foot or foot-bandage for Oedipus

Props

- 'microphone' (optional)
- file-cards (optional)
- 3 rostra (optional)
- 3 buzzers or noise-makers of some kind
- gaudy placard or archway saying THE GREAT THE-BAN QUIZ SHOW
- Sphinx head could be made up by several actors holding her separate features on long canes, i.e., eyes, snout, mouth, mane . . .

Special Effects

- amplified voice, roar and noises of Sphinx supplied from offstage (could use voice-changer)

• TV-quiz-style theme music/fanfare; loud clock ticking; raspberry sound

Idea!

Did you know? Oedipus (who was abandoned at birth and never knew his parents) has unwittingly killed his father and is now, unknowingly, about to marry his own mother. As a result of this sin, plague hits Thebes and everything ends unhappily for absolutely everybody. Not many laughs there.

THE RIDDLE OF THE SPHINX

3 rostra are ranged aslant the left-hand side of the stage. A glitzy archway or placard trumpets the words THE GREAT THEBAN QUIZ SHOW. Brash TV style. The CONTESTANTS RED, BLUE *and* YELLOW *stand each at a rostrum, manning a buzzer – say one bell, one bicycle horn, one quacker. The* QUEEN *and* PRIME MINISTER *lurk anxiously at the back.*

(*Enter* QUIZMASTER *with microphone, file-cards and loud fanfare of inane music*)

QUIZMASTER: Welcome back to THE GREAT THEBAN QUIZ SHOW and a wonderful bunch of contestants! And it's hands on buzzers for the next round. Why – I said – why did the Cyclops give up teaching?

RED: Because it wasn't worth going on with just one pupil!

(*Fanfare*)

QUIZMASTER: Correct – I can see you're in good form tonight! Next question! What – I said – what do you get if you cross a crocodile with a lettuce?

BLUE: A Caesar's salad?

QUIZMASTER: It's good but it's not good enough . . . Yes, Yellow!

YELLOW: A big green salad that eats you?

(*Fanfare*)

QUIZMASTER: Ah, these people are so bright I could see them in the dark. Next question! What – I said – what flies without going anywhere?

BLUE: A flag!

(*Ribald fanfare*)

QUIZMASTER: Ah, and now the one we've all been waiting for, and who's going to be the lucky one tonight? With a lead of two points – step forward please – it's your big moment . . . RED!

(*Manhandles* RED *into position centre-stage*)

You've won yourself a trip for one to a spot just down the road from this studio. Once you get there you'll have your chance to find out if your answer was correct. All right? Nervous? Don't be. We're right behind you. Are you ready? Here we go, then! What – I said – what goes on four legs in the morning, two legs in the afternoon, three in the evening, and is weakest when it has most?

RED: Is it an octopus at a fishmarket, Ray?

QUIZMASTER: Well, let's find out, shall we? Off you go now and (ALL *join in with catchphrase*) THE BEST OF THEBAN LUCK!

(*Exit* RED. *Loud ticking of a clock. Squawking raspberry noise*)

Well, that's how it goes, folks. That wasn't the answer. Our star prize is still up there. And tomorrow night – who knows? – it could be yours. So let's hear from you if you want to play THE GREAT THEBAN QUIZ SHOW. Until then . . . THE BEST OF THEBAN LUCK!

(*Brash music grinds to a halt.* CONTESTANTS *and* QUIZMASTER *freeze*)

QUEEN JOCASTA: (*moving downstage with* PRIME MINIS-TER) Any news?

PRIME MINISTER: Nothing.

QUEEN JOCASTA: Any new ideas?

PRIME MINISTER: None.

QUEEN JOCASTA: What more can we do? What more can I offer as a reward but my own hand in marriage – the crown of Thebes itself!

PRIME MINISTER: The stakes are just too high.

QUIZMASTER: It's not that people aren't tempted.

PRIME MINISTER: It's just that they *don't know*.

(QUEEN *and* PRIME MINISTER *retire. Quiz show comes back to life. Enter* GREEN *to take place of* RED)

QUIZMASTER: Hands on buzzers, now! What – I said – what has the head of a woman, the body of a lion and the wings of an eagle?

BLUE: Is it the Sphinx of Thebes, Ray?

QUIZMASTER: Correct! Now for a bonus point can anyone tell me what the – I said – what the Sphinx eats?

YELLOW: Oo. I think I know this, Ray! Is it people who can't answer her riddle?

QUIZMASTER: Is the right answer! And that makes it time for *The Big One*. Now remember, everyone, you could go home from here today King of Thebes. Yes, Green! Are you going to challenge?

GREEN: No, no. 'Sno good.

YELLOW: (*buzzing*) I'll give it a go, Ray!

QUIZMASTER: That's the ticket! Let's have a big hand for a good sport. Here it is, then. *The Big One*. Take your time.

What goes on four legs in the morning, two legs in the afternoon, three in the evening, and is weakest when it has most?

YELLOW: Is it one of the constellations, Ray?

QUIZMASTER: Sounds good to me. Come with me and let's find out if you're right. And THE BEST OF THEBAN LUCK!

> (*Escorts her off stage. Roar, scuffle, slavering noise.* QUIZMASTER *re-enters covering his mouth, looking dreadful*)

ALL ON STAGE: Well?

> (QUIZMASTER *shakes his head. Show freezes*)

QUEEN JOCASTA: We should try to get a message out. Try to summon help. Our allies could send an army to destroy her. They could at least break through with food. The people are starting to starve!

PRIME MINISTER: There's only one road through that pass. Ravines on both sides. The Sphinx can stop and question every soul who passes through. She has us completely cut off.

QUIZMASTER: (*serious, unsmiling*) And why? For the sake of a riddle – a joke – a trick question – a 'poser' – a puzzle. Why? Why us? Why Thebes? . . . No, no. You don't have to answer. Just a rhetorical question.

> (*Show comes back to life.* NEW YELLOW *take the place of previous* YELLOW)

BLUE: (*buzzing*) Is it one of the gods?

GREEN: (*buzzing*) Is it a chimera?

NEW YELLOW: (*buzzing*) Is it some kind of a knot?

BLUE: (*buzzing*) Is it the Oracle at Delphi?

GREEN: (*buzzing*) Is it a windmill?

NEW YELLOW: (*buzzing*) Is it a thundercloud?

GREEN: (*buzzing*) A watersport?

BLUE: A relay race?

QUIZMASTER: Well let's find out, shall we? It's time to *Ask the Sphinx*! So off you go and . . . THE BEST OF THEBAN LUCK!

(*Exit* CONTESTANTS)

You poor fools.

QUEEN JOCASTA: The streets of Thebes are emptier every day. We used to have our fair share of know-alls. Every town does. Our fair share of lunatics, and greedy chancers . . . and heroes . . . and desperadoes.

PRIME MINISTER: They've all gone now. No one left. They've all taken their chance with the Sphinx and been peeled like oranges.

QUEEN JOCASTA: Torn into segments like oranges.

PRIME MINISTER: Squeezed and eaten like oranges.

QUISMASTER: *What does she want with us, this she-devil?* . . . No. It's all right. You don't have to answer. It was a rhetorical question.

PRIME MINISTER: No one knows the answer to the Riddle of the Sphinx.

(*Re-enter* CONTESTANTS, *this time as* CITIZENS, *sharing lines*)

CITIZENS: We rack our brains. / We scour our books. / We pray to the gods to enlighten us. / We starve, besieged by the beastly Sphinx. / No one can leave the city. / No one can reach it either.

QUIZMASTER: You could say, we are all dying of ignorance.

(*Exit* ALL.

Enter OEDIPUS, *limping up the centre aisle, whistling between his teeth. Deafening pre-recorded roar. The* SPHINX's *head emerges, huge and menacing. Her voice is amplified throughout*)

SPHINX: Stand, traveller, and answer me!

OEDIPUS: Well I never. There's different. How can I help? Think on, mind. I'm a stranger in these parts.

SPHINX: (*breathing noisily*) Answer me this riddle!

OEDIPUS: Oh. Righto. I'll give it a go. Ask away, lass. Run it by me.

SPHINX: Who are you?

OEDIPUS: Is that the question? That's easy. Name's Oedipus (with an O.E.). Satisfactory? Good. I'll toddle along, then. Am I going the right way for Thebes, by the by?

SPHINX: I am the Sphinx and my blood is sorrow! My heart is wrath and my brain is turmoil!

OEDIPUS: There, there. Don't be hard on yourself, lass. You've got a pretty face.

SPHINX: Answer this riddle, or I shall tear you as I have torn all those before you, and scatter your bones in the ravine below!

OEDIPUS: Now, now, lass. I can see you're not entirely happy within yourself. I can tell these things.

SPHINX: What goes on four legs in the morning, two legs in the afternoon, three in the evening, and is weakest when it has most?

OEDIPUS: Oh! That old one! Heard it.

(*Great roar from the* SPHINX)

Oh! You want me to tell you the answer? Sorry! I thought you knew it. I thought everyone knew that old chestnut. (*To the audience*) You know it, don't you?

(*Another roar*)

Steady on! Righto, lass. What goes on four legs in the morning, two in the afternoon, and three in the evening?

(*The* SPHINX *lurches at him. In the nick of time he says:*)

It's a Man, that's what!

(SPHINX *recoils.* OEDIPUS *mimes*)

Goes on all fours when he's a babby; walks on two legs when he's full grown; leans on a stick in his dotage. Now, if that's all: am I set right for Thebes, did you say?

(SPHINX *sways her head, reels, staggers, howls then goes. Rest of* CAST *creep on stage from either side, at the back*)

Ooo, look at that, now. She's jumped clear into the ravine. Poor lass. Bit drastic, that, all over a riddle. Beautiful face she had. But sad. Terrible sad. It's quite dampened me spirits, that has. (*Shakes himself*) Can't be helped.

PRIME MINISTER: (*calling*) Hey, you! Where did you come from? How did you get through?

OEDIPUS: From Corinth, me. Oedipus is the name. With an O.E.

PRIME MINISTER: Did the Sphinx not stop you on the road?

OEDIPUS: Something of that sort. She took it amiss when I answered her riddle. Went and heaved herself over a cliff. Is this Thebes?

QUEEN JOCASTA: It is, sir, and you are most welcome! – to your prize . . . to your crown (*presents crown*) . . . and to me. (*Curtseys*)

OEDIPUS: Way-hey-hey! (*To* JOCASTA – *who is really his mother*) Haven't I seen your face somewhere? It's dead familiar.

QUIZMASTER: (*to audience*) Let's have a big hand now for the new King of Thebes. He has lifted the siege and answered the Riddle of the Sphinx! With such a King, married to our own dear Queen Jocasta, what can *possibly* go wrong?

(CONTESTANTS *rush to their rostra. All the buzzers sound, long and loud*)

Please, please! Ladies and gentlemen! It was a purely rhetorical question!

(*He begins the cheering as* OEDIPUS *and the* QUEEN *process off followed by rest of cast who chant:*)

ALL: Hail Oedipus Rex. Hail Oedipus Rex! Hail Oedipus Rex! [etc.]

Breaking the Bonds

Even after Herakles has worked out his sentence of hard labour, he has one more feat to perform on behalf of humankind.

Cast

KING EURYSTHEUS

HERAKLES

OBSERVER

ATLAS (a giant)

4 SKY SUPPORTERS

    APHRODITE

    HERMES

    HERA

    ZEUS

    other GODS as desired

PROMETHEUS

EAGLE OPERATORS

PANDORA*

SISYPHUS*

ODYSSEUS*

HEPHAESTUS*

HE and SHE*

GIRLFRIEND*

CHORUS*

WHOLE CAST to end

Costumes

• shaggy, grassy poncho for Atlas

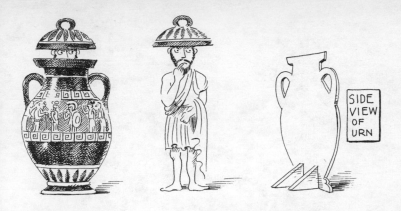

Props

- cut-out of urn
- lid-hat for King
- 3 golden apples
- sky on 4 canes
- box/bench for Atlas to stand on
- Prometheus's chains*
- eagle mitts*
- butterfly of Hope*
- Sisyphus's boulder*

*These characters (and their props) are only needed if the whole script is used. Use only those who have appeared in your chosen programme of plays.

Special Effects

- crashing, breaking glass, etc.

Idea!

There are alternative ends to these plays. Which will you choose? Can you think of a third alternative?

BREAKING THE BONDS

The miniature figure of PROMETHEUS *(still) hangs from its chains in the background. A large, two-dimensional urn stands centre-stage. Its lid is a hat worn by* KING EURYSTHEUS, *who stands hidden behind it.*

KING: (*his head rising into view*) Is he back yet? Is he here? My nerves are in rags. I don't know how much more of this I can take. I'm in fragments. Cooped up in here like a message in a bottle. Ye gods! I thought it would be so droll having a demi-god at my beck and call! (*Emerging further into sight to begin narrative*) I was given the job of punishing him, you see. Herakles. 'Go and serve King Eurystheus for ten years': that was the sentence of the gods. I was willing – well, willing and eager, if I'm honest. I like inflicting pain.

So I send him here, there and all over, doing the kind of horrible jobs no one else will do – *can* do! He gets rid of the Nemean Lion and the Stymphalian cranes. Useful, that. Cleans out the Augean stables when they're stinking out the countryside. Phew! . . . Then I begin to think, 'There must be a profit to be made here, somewhere, Eurystheus,' and I send him off to catch the Golden Hind and steal the jewelled belt of the Amazon Queen. Well, why not? You don't get the use of a demi-god with superhuman strength every day of the week. What would you do with one? But that Herakles: he's so . . . morose, you know? Never smiles. Looks right through you. Pretty soon I'm giving him tasks just hoping he'll get killed. But even the Hydra couldn't finish him off. He just kept coming back. And scowling at me. I got this urn made to keep him off me . . . Is he out there? Is he coming? I'm supposed to be his gaoler and look at me! He's out there and I'm in here. I must think of something truly impossible . . . something that will take him months to achieve – a journey. Yes! A journey to the top of the world!

(*Enter* HERAKLES. EURYSTHEUS *ducks down in terror*)

HERAKLES: I've captured the Great Oxen of Erytheia. What do you want me to do with them?

KING: You mean you *brought them back with you*?

(*Huge, long, crashing and breaking noises offstage*)

He brought them back with him . . . Well, set them free again before they wreck my palace!

(HERAKLES *turns to go*)

and then . . .

(HERAKLES *turns back*)

(*gabbling*) And then fetch me three golden apples from the Orchard of the Hesperides. (*Ducks down*)

HERAKLES: The what? (*Goes and knocks on urn*) The what?

KING: No! Don't kill me! I forbid it! It's not allowed!

HERAKLES: Fetch what?

KING: Three apples from the Gardens of the Hesperides!

(HERAKLES *knocks again*)

Go away! Leave me alone! Guards!

HERAKLES: Where are they, these Gardens?

KING: At the top of the world, of course, you ignoramus! Now go!

(*Exit* HERAKLES. KING EURYSTHEUS *emerges mopping his brow; another lucky escape*)

And guarded by a dragon – BIG dragon – BIG BIG dragon that eats demi-gods like so much falafel. Tee hee hee. That should get you out of my hair once and for all, Herakles.

(*The* KING *picks up his urn and goes.*

Enter HERAKLES)

HERAKLES: Long way to the top of the world. And then when I get there . . . (*Gives a great groan and sits down, addressing audience*) I'm weary. Weary to my very soul. Oh, not from the Labours. Not from running Eurystheus's petty errands for him. Just weary of . . . *being*. Look. There hangs Prometheus, chained to the mountains, the eagles gouging and tearing at him day after day. I know how you feel, my friend! My own guilty conscience is tearing at my insides like that. (*Stands up to confess*) My name is Herakles, and I am an alcoholic.

Oh, I only drank once, but that was enough. In my stupor I killed my darling wife and children. What could Eurystheus do to me that I wouldn't welcome? (*Spreads his arms so that he looks like* PROMETHEUS) What did you ever do wrong, Prometheus? Nothing! Nothing but steal fire for the sake of your little Family of Man. But me . . . It should be me up there, not you. What's my punishment? Another *shopping* trip for Eurystheus. Pah! (*Sits down again, calmer*) The Orchard of the Hesperides. Long way to go just to scrump apples. Also, I've no idea where it is. I think I'll ask Atlas. The Hesperides are his daughters, after all.

(*Behind him four* CANE-BEARERS *enter supporting a sagging canopy of black silky material: 'the night sky'. Enter* ATLAS, *who stands on a box, supporting the silk on his hands and shoulders*)

HERAKLES: (*turning and calling upwards*) Hoi there, Atlas! A word if you please!

ATLAS: Any number. I die of boredom here all alone, holding up the sky.

HERAKLES: Is the sky heavy?

ATLAS: Is the sky heavy? Why do people always ask me that? Tourists, scientists, children on school trips . . . 'Is the sky heavy?' A trillion fathoms of firmament crammed with stars and planets and cosmic dust? An ocean of air burdened with birds and studded with thunderclaps? A tidal wave of dark perpetually breaking over my back? Why would it be heavy?

. . . It's a job. Someone has to do it.

HERAKLES: I am on my way north to visit relations of yours. Your daughters the Hesperides.

ATLAS: My daughters? Oh, lucky man! What I'd give to see them! Tell them I love them and miss them . . . I hope you don't expect to go inside the gates. No mortal is allowed inside, you know. Those apple trees belong to the gods.

HERAKLES: Now that's a terrible shame. Because I need to fetch three of its golden apples for my master. Have you been there yourself?

ATLAS: How would I? I've been standing here since long before the Gardens were even planted. Pity. When I was young I thought I'd like to travel. And to see my daughters after all this time!

HERAKLES: You should go.

ATLAS: And whales should play the zither, but they don't.

HERAKLES: Every prisoner deserves parole. Perhaps you could get someone to stand in for you.

ATLAS: STAND IN FOR ME? HA! The man's not born who could do it.

HERAKLES: (*after long pause*) I could.

ATLAS: YOU!? (*Laughs hugely*)

HERAKLES: (*to audience*) On the other side of the world,

meteorites crash to earth and rainbows snag on the trees. Atlas the Giant is laughing. Not a thing he has done for ten thousand years. (*To* ATLAS) I've heard your story, Atlas. How the gods punished you like this for stirring up rebellion. First you . . . then Prometheus. What tyrants they are, the gods. It should be you going on this journey, not me.

ATLAS: You're right! It should be me! . . . Could you really do it? Just for a day?

HERAKLES: They say I'm the strongest mortal who ever lived . . . But I wouldn't get my apples then, would I?

ATLAS: (*preoccupied*) Oh, I could fetch you the apples. Apples aren't a problem. My daughters would give them to me . . .

HERAKLES: It's a deal, then! I hold up the sky while you visit the top of the world. Then we swap back.

(*They change places.* HERAKLES *makes much of the weight, staggering, buckling, bracing himself, grimacing.* ATLAS *savours his freedom, stretching, jumping, running round stage, then off*)

The sky's hanging lower tonight. Like a tent with snow on its roof. The moon looks larger, the stars as big as flakes of ash. Can you feel the earth trembling? That's Atlas running. He's wading oceans now, vaulting over mountain ranges to reach the gardens at the top of the world.

Here it is, then. This is it. The Labour that's too hard. The impossible task. Zeus, but these stars are burning – like a million candles stubbed out against my back! My spine is crumbling like a stick of chalk! My veins are bursting! My joints are fusing into stone! The sky will crush me!

Where is Atlas? Why doesn't he come? Ah well. At last I've found a punishment equal to my crime. The sky will crush me into sand and I shall be nothing and nowhere and nobody. *Where is Atlas?* This is how it must have been for

Prometheus. All these years. Generation to generation. Waiting to be rescued from the pain— At last!

(*Re-enter* ATLAS)

Did you bring them? The apples?

ATLAS: (*capering, playing with the apples*) I did, I did. Here they are. Was I gone long?

HERAKLES: No time at all.

ATLAS: I got thinking on the way. I've lost my taste for this business. Time to *delegate*. I've decided, Herakles, to let *you* go on holding up the sky.

(*Long pause*)

HERAKLES: Fine. Good. It's a privilege.

ATLAS: You don't mind?

HERAKLES: Not a bit. It's lighter than I expected. Not much more than a big-brimmed hat, really. You go. I'll be fine . . . Only . . . take the apples to King Eurystheus, will you, and make my excuses?

ATLAS: Why not? Happy to oblige!

(ATLAS *goes to leave*)

HERAKLES: Oh and . . . just before you go— Help me put a pad across my shoulders, will you? These stars. Like nettles the way they prickle.

ATLAS: A pad?

HERAKLES: A pad.

ATLAS: They do prickle, don't they? A pad, yes. Why did I never think of that? How . . .

HERAKLES: You just steady the sky a moment while I . . . Here, let me hold those for you . . . (*takes golden apples*) Got it? Got your balance?

(They again laboriously change places. HERAKLES *somersaults away, punching the air, exultant)*

ATLAS: What are you doing? Where are you going?

HERAKLES: Oh. It's just that I've changed my mind. I've decided to let *you* go on holding up the sky. Since the gods set you the task. Who am I to alter Fate?

(Exit HERAKLES *laughing.* ATLAS *gives a great groan of despair.*

Those supporting the sky let the front edge drop down so that ATLAS *is hidden. He discreetly leaves and* PROMETHEUS *takes his place. The mini-Prometheus is removed.*

Enter KING EURYSTHEUS *running, carrying his urn, in a panic)*

KING: It's like throwing a stick for a dog. He keeps coming

back for more! Shall I never be rid of this dog Herakles? I've even sent him to Hell, but he just came back like a ghost to haunt me! Pardon him, you gods! For pity sake – NO MORE LABOURS OF HERAKLES!

(*Runs off other side. Enter the* GODS *in a bunch, sharing lines*)

THE GODS: His Labours are complete./
Herakles has served his sentence./
We never thought he would./
We never thought he could./

APHRODITE: So strong, Herakles. So very . . . powerful.

HERMES: And cunning, too.

HERA: (*scowling at* ZEUS) You would almost think he had immortal blood in him.

ZEUS: (*extending arms in welcome*) My boy!

(*Enter* HERAKLES *who looks across but does not move towards the* GODS)

HERAKLES: One last thing to do. One last Labour of my own. One last epic journey – to the Mountains of the Caucasus this time. One demi-god seeking out another.

(*Exit* GODS. SKY-HOLDERS *go, revealing behind them* PROMETHEUS *(live), chained, arms outstretched. He is tormented by actors wearing the eagle-mitts (see –* Stolen Fire)

A thousand years ago, the gods punished Prometheus for stealing the secret of fire and giving it to Man. I deserved my hard labour – but not he, not this, not Prometheus. He simply wounded the pride of the gods by loving Humankind more than them.

PROMETHEUS: Between sky and earth I stand, like Atlas. From up here I can see a hundred miles into the distance – a thousand years into the past. But I can see no end to my pain. Like Atlas. An eternity of pain.

PANDORA: (*holding the butterfly Hope*) There's always Hope, Prometheus.

SISYPHUS: (*carrying his boulder*) There's always the *possibility* of escape.

HE AND SHE: And prayers, Prometheus. All these years we have been praying for you!

HEPHAESTUS: And the gods are changeable, Prometheus. They quickly lose interest in their sport.

(ZEUS *crosses stage with a new* GIRLFRIEND)

ODYSSEUS: There are always us Heroes, ducking and diving our way to glory.

CHORUS: There's an end to every story, Prometheus. Happy or sad. A story never ends up in the air.

(*To audience*)

You creatures whom Prometheus made from clay:
His fate now rests with you: what do you say?

HERAKLES: (*to audience*) What do YOU say? It was you he stole for. Shall I free him?

(*He breaks the chains, in answer to the audience saying so*)

CHORUS: What can they do, the gods who hung him there?
What can they do but shrug and fume and stare.
Like the cloud-banks changing ceaselessly,
NOTHING lasts for all Eternity.

(*Exit* ALL)

Ons and Offs

This is extra material to be used when you are putting several plays together to make a performance. The introduction to the second half would suit a programme devised to give a first half devoted to the gods and a second half to mortals. If you assemble it in some different way you may want to write an alternative second-half introduction.

The extra material is in four parts: an opening chorus, a chorus to close the first half, a chorus to open the second half and a choice of two endings for the whole performance.

Ons and Offs

To use at the beginning of a performance

CHORUS: (*wearing Greek drama mask*)
Before the concrete came the flowers.
Before this time of yours came ours.
Before the first bare man was made,
Rose the Olympians' palisade,
Out where the sun-bleached mountains cool
Their feet in the Mediterranean pool.
After the Titans' tyranny
Came the Olympian victory.

(ALL *cheer*)

CHORUS: (*with* CAST *responding*) Give me an O – L – Y!
Give me an M – P – I!
Give me an A – N – S!
What've we got?

REST OF CAST: OLYMPIANS!!

CHORUS: Once the battle flags were furled,
Four brothers carved the roasted world:

(*Introduces them one by one*)

Poseidon!

POSEIDON: Storms and shoals and ships for me!
I rule the world-encircled sea!

CHORUS: Pluto!

PLUTO: In inky hall that even sunlight fled,
I rule the infernal kingdom of the Dead!

CHORUS: Helios!

HELIOS: Give me Sun's fiery chariot to fly
And I will rule the Kingdom of the Sky!

CHORUS: But there on Mount Olympus' cloudy peak
Sits one of whom all storytellers speak:
Dreaming of you and me he sits and nods . . .
ZEUS, THE ALMIGHTY FATHER OF THE GODS!

To use at the end of the first half

HERMES *or* CHORUS: Once Pegasus, in riding through the skies,
Clipped Olympus with his hooves and so gave rise
To Hippocras – to wine – the very first
Ever to slake an honest mortal's thirst.
So we thank the gods we have a thirst to slake!
We'll see you all again after the break!

REST OF CAST: YASSAS!

To use at the beginning of the second half

CHORUS: Welcome back to summer climes!
Welcome back to Ancient Times!

(*This time the* CAST *does not respond to the cheerleading*)

Give me an O – L – Y!
Give me an M – P – I!
Give me an A – N – S!
What've we got?

(*Silence*)

What's this? Dyslexia? (*Silence*) Mutiny?

VARIOUS MEMBERS OF CAST: The gods can be pretty spiteful. / They don't exactly encourage private initiative, do they? / One step out of place and they wax all wrathful, don't they? / Hurling thunderbolts. / Transforming people into spiders and bulls and flowers!

CHORUS: So what do we show them instead?

SISYPHUS *or* ODYSSEUS: (*nervously at first*) Give us a G. Give us an R. Give us an E – E – K – S. What do you get?

REST OF CAST: HEROES!

To use at the end (version A)

CHORUS: So many heroes still to come,
So many heroes still unsung.
Would there were time for us to show
The Argonauts, Arachne and Echo—

REST OF CAST: Echo – Echo – Echo

CHORUS: Sphinxes, sirens, whirlpools, Minotaurs
And wine-dark seas cut by a thousand oars.
Like mad Cassandra picturing Troy alight,
We would dazzle you with too much sight.
As many as the feathers in a wing
Are the myths and legends we could sing,
But we know better than to stay too long;
The wax that binds us may not prove so strong.
So we resign to you the open sky.
Please don't try to fly too high – GOODBYE!

REST OF CAST: Icarus, NO! Don't do it, Icarus! Look out! No!

ICARUS: (*bursting through* CAST *from behind, opening wings and leaping off front of stage to run down auditorium*) WHEEEEEEEEE!!!!!

Alternative ending: A brief farewell

CHORUS: Olympus' peak is covered now with snow;
Nothing of thrones or marble pavements show.
Higher up they've gone – higher than high,
Leaving their silent footprints on the sky.
The Olympians roam the topless towers of night,
Their shapes pricked out in a million starry lights.

THE GODS: And so GOODNIGHT!

ALL MORTALS: GOODNIGHT!

EVERYONE: GOODNIGHT!